Books
Phrase Book
Victoria Alvarez and Jillian Norman

Spanish Phrase Book

María Victoria Alvarez and Jillian Norman

Penguin Books Ltd, Harmondsworth,
Middlesex, England
Penguin Books Inc., 7110 Ambassador Road,
Baltimore, Maryland 21207, U.S.A.
Penguin Books Australia Ltd, Ringwood,
Victoria, Australia
Penguin Books Canada Ltd, 41 Steelcase Road West,
Markham, Ontario, Canada
Penguin Books (N.Z.) Ltd, 182–190 Wairau Road,
Auckland 10, New Zealand

First published 1968
Reprinted 1969, 1970, 1971, 1972, 1973 (twice), 1974
Copyright © Jillian Norman and Maria Victoria Alvarez, 1968

Made and printed in Great Britain by
Hazell Watson & Viney Ltd, Aylesbury, Bucks
Set in Monotype Plantin

CONTENTS

Contents

INTRODUCTION

In this series of phrase books only those words and phrases that are essential to the traveller have been included. For easy reference the phrases are divided into several sections, each one dealing with a different situation. Some of the Spanish phrases are marked with an asterisk – these attempt to give an indication of the kind of reply you may get to your questions.

At the end of the book is an extensive vocabulary list and here a pronunciation guide is given for each word. In addition there is an explanation of Spanish pronunciation at the beginning of the book and a brief survey of the essential points of grammar. It would be advisable to read these sections before starting to use the book.

Tape recordings

For those who would like to study the phrases and perfect their pronunciation, a further aid is available in the form of two 90-minute tapes or cassettes which contain all the words and phrases spoken clearly and distinctly by a Spaniard.

A leaflet giving full details is available from the Institute of Tape Learning, P.O. Box 180, London NW3 3JL (Telephone 01-722 3314).

PANISH PRONUNCIATION

e pronunciation guide is intended for people with no knowledge of
nish. As far as possible the system is based on English pronuncia-
1. This means that complete accuracy may sometimes be lost for
sake of simplicity, but the reader should be able to understand
nish pronunciation, and make himself understood, if he reads this
tion carefully. In addition, each word in the vocabulary is given with
ronunciation guide.

wels

Spanish vowel sounds are pure, they are not slurred as in English.
al e is always pronounced.

nounce a as **a** in father	Symbol **a**	e.g. casa – house (ka-sa)	
e as **e** in bed	Symbol **e**	e.g. negro – black (ne-gro)	
nd as **ai** in air	Symbol **ai**, **ay**	e.g. poder – to be able (po-dair)	
i as **i** in machine	Symbol **ee**	e.g. fin – end (feen)	
o as **o** in porter	Symbol **o(h)**	e.g. todo – all (toh-doh)	
u as **oo** in boot	Symbol **oo**	e.g. mucho – much (moo-cho)	

mpound vowels

the groups ia, ie, io the **i** sound resembles **y** in yes	Symbol **y**, **ee**	e.g. alguien – anyone (alg-yen)
the groups ue, ui, uo the **u** sound resembles **w** as in wet	Symbol **w**, **oo**	e.g. bueno – good (bwe-no).

Consonants

Many are similar to English consonants but note the following:

c before e or i is pronounced **th** as in thin	Symbol **th**	e.g. cerrar – to shut (ther-rar)
c before a, o, u or a consonant is pronounced **k**	Symbol **k**	e.g. coche – car (ko-che)
final **d** is not always pronounced		e.g. edad – age (ai-da
g before e or i is pronounced like English **h** (hot) or Scottish **ch** (loch)	Symbol **h**	e.g. gente – people (hen-te)
g before a, o, u or a consonant is pronounced **g** as in got	Symbol **g**	e.g. gafas – glasses (ga-fas)
h is always silent		
j is like English **h** (hot) or Scottish **ch** (loch)	Symbol **h**	e.g. mujer – woman (moo-hair)
ll is like **lli** in million	Symbol **lly**	e.g. llamar – to call (llya-mar)
ñ is like **ni** in onion	Symbol **ny**	e.g. mañana – morni (ma-nya-na)
q(u) is pronounced as **k**	Symbol **k**	e.g. queso – cheese (ke-so)
r is trilled, **rr** trilled even more strongly		
v is pronounced as **b**	Symbol **b**	e.g. vaso – glass (ba-so)
z is pronounced **th** as in thin	Symbol **th**	e.g. manzana – apple (man-tha-na)

is is the pronunciation used in Spain. In Spanish America there are
or two differences, notably **c** + **e** or **i** and **z** are pronounced **s**
th.

ess

rds ending in a vowel, **n** or **s** are stressed on the last syllable but
: **casa**, **gafas**, **ven**den.

rds ending in a consonant other than **n** or **s** are stressed on the
syllable: ha**blar**, espa**ñol**.

ceptions to these rules are indicated by a written accent: café,
obús, estación. In the pronunciation guide, words with irregular
ess have the stressed syllable printed in bold.

ESSENTIAL GRAMMAR

NOUNS

Nouns in Spanish are either masculine or feminine.
Nouns denoting males are masculine, as are most nouns ending in **-o**.
Nouns denoting females are feminine, as are most nouns ending in **-a.**

    e.g. tío – uncle; vaso – glass; tía – aunt; playa – beach.

Plural

The plural is formed by adding **-s** if the word ends in a vowel; **-es**
if it ends in a consonant.

    e.g. peseta – pesetas; tren (train) – trenes.

DEFINITE ARTICLE – the

el before a masculine singular noun	el banco (the bank)
los before a masculine plural noun	los bancos
la before a feminine singular noun	la peseta
las before a feminine plural noun	las pesetas

INDEFINITE ARTICLE – a, an

un before a masculine singular noun	un banco
una before a feminine singular noun	una peseta

ADJECTIVES

Adjectives agree in number and gender with the noun.
Those ending in **-o** change to **-a** in the feminine.

    e.g. fresco – fresca (fresh, cool).

Those ending in **-e** and most of those ending in a consonant are the same in the masculine and the feminine.

e.g. el coche grande; la casa grande.

The plural is formed by adding **-s** if the word ends in a vowel, **-es** if it ends in a consonant.

e.g. fresco – frescos; azul (blue) – azules.

The comparative and superlative are formed by putting **más** before the adjective.

e.g. un hotel barato   a cheap hotel
un hotel más barato   a cheaper hotel
el hotel más barato de la ciudad   the cheapest hotel in the town

POSSESSIVE ADJECTIVES

	s	*pl*
my	mi	mis
your (*fam.*)	tu	tus
his, her	su	sus
their, your (*polite*)	su	sus
our	nuestro	nuestros
your (*fam.*)	vuestro	vuestros

These adjectives agree with the thing possessed, e.g. mi casa (my house); mis casas (my houses); vuestro libro (your book); vuestra carta (your letter).

PERSONAL PRONOUNS

	subject	*object*
I	yo	me
you (*fam.*)	tú	te
you (*polite*)	usted	le (*m*), la (*f*)
he	él	le
she	ella	la
it	él/ella	lo
we	nosotros/-as	nos
you (*fam.*)	vosotros/-as	os
you (*polite*)	ustedes	los (*m*), las (*f*)
they *m*	ellos	los
they *f*	ellas	las

Personal pronouns are usually omitted before the verb.
  e.g. voy – I go; viene – he (she) comes.

Direct object pronouns are usually placed before the verb.
  e.g. me ve – he sees me.

Indirect object pronouns are the same as direct object pronouns except that **le** is used to mean to him, to her, to it, to you (*polite*), and **les** means to them and to you (*polite*). If a direct and an indirect object pronoun are used together, the indirect one is placed first.
  e.g. me lo da – he gives it to me.

If both pronouns are in the third person, **se** is used as indirect objec
   e.g. se lo da – he gives it to him.

When speaking to strangers always use the forms **usted** and **ustede**
Tú and **vosotros** are used to close friends and to children.

DEMONSTRATIVE PRONOUNS

this one, that one

	m	*f*
this (one)	éste	ésta
these	éstos	éstas
that (one)	ése	ésa
those	ésos	ésas
that (one) over there	aquél	aquélla
those	aquéllos	aquéllas

They agree in number and gender with the nouns they represent
   e.g. éste es mi bolígrafo – this is my ball-point.

      quiero esta postal, ésa, y aquélla – I want this postcard, that on
      and that one over there.

The demonstrative adjectives have the same form as the pronoun
except that they are not written with accents.

VERBS

'To be' is translated by **ser** and **estar**.

When it is followed by a noun, or when it indicates an origin, or a permanent or inherent quality, **ser** is used.

e.g. la nieve es fría y blanca	snow is cold and white
soy inglés	I am English
Inglaterra es una isla	England is an island

When it indicates position or a temporary state, **estar** is used.

e.g. el hotel está en la calle principal	the hotel is in the main street
estamos en España	we are in Spain

Present tense of **ser** and **estar**

	ser	*estar*
I am	soy	estoy
you are	eres	estás
he, she is,	es	está
you are	es	está
we are	somos	estamos
you are	sois	estáis
they, you are	son	están

'To have, to possess' is translated by **tener.**

I have, etc.	tengo
	tienes
	tiene
	tenemos

> tenéis
> tienen

e.g. tengo mi pasaporte – I have my passport.

'To have' = **haber** is only used to form compound tenses of other verbs.

e.g. he visto el hotel – I've seen the hotel.

I have, etc.   he
               has
               ha
               hemos
               habéis
               han

In Spanish there are three types of verbs, distinguished by the endings of the infinitives.

e.g. **-ar**   hablar – to speak
     -er   vender – to sell
     -ir   vivir – to live

The present tense is formed as follows:

hablar	*vender*	*vivir*
hablo	vendo	vivo
hablas	vendes	vives
habla	vende	vive
hablamos	vendemos	vivimos
habláis	vendéis	vivís
hablan	venden	viven

The present tense of some common irregular verbs:

dar, to give	*decir*, to say	*hacer*, to do, make
doy	digo	hago
das	dices	haces
da	dice	hace
damos	decimos	hacemos
dais	decís	hacéis
dan	dicen	hacen

ir, to go	*poder*, can, to be able	*poner*, to put
voy	puedo	pongo
vas	puedes	pones
va	puede	pone
vamos	podemos	ponemos
vais	podéis	ponéis
van	pueden	ponen

querer, to want, to love	*traer*, to bring	*venir*, to come
quiero	traigo	vengo
quieres	traes	vienes
quiere	trae	viene
queremos	traemos	venimos
queréis	traéis	venís
quieren	traen	vienen

The past participle is formed by dropping the infinitive ending and
adding the following endings to the stem of the verb.

-ar	hablar – to speak	**-ado**	hablado – spoken
-er	vender – to sell	**-ido**	vendido – sold
-ir	vivir – to live	**-ido**	vivido – lived

Some common irregular past participles:
abierto from abrir – opened
dicho from decir – said
escrito from escribir – written
hecho from hacer – made, done
puesto from poner – put
visto from ver – seen

The imperfect tense

	hablar		*vender*
I was speaking,	habl**aba**	I was selling,	vend**ía**
used to speak,	habl**abas**	used to sell,	vend**ías**
spoke, etc.	habl**aba**	sold, etc.	vend**ía**
	habl**ábamos**		vend**íamos**
	habl**abais**		vend**íais**
	habl**aban**		vend**ían**

Verbs ending in **-ir** (vivir) have the same endings in the imperfect as those in **-er** (vender).

Irregular imperfect tense of **ser** – to be
era
eras
era
éramos
erais
eran

The future is formed by adding the following endings to the infinitives of all regular verbs:

hablar	*vender*	*vivir*
hablar**é**	vender**é**	vivir**é**
hablar**ás**	vender**ás**	vivir**ás**
hablar**á**	vender**á**	vivir**á**
hablar**emos**	vender**emos**	vivir**emos**
hablar**éis**	vender**éis**	vivir**éis**
hablar**án**	vender**án**	vivir**án**

The negative is formed by putting **no** before the verb.
    e.g. no hablo español – I don't speak Spanish.

FIRST THINGS

Essentials

Yes	Sí
No	No
Please	Por favor
Thank you	Gracias
No thank you	No gracias

Questions and requests

Where is/are ...?	¿Dónde está/están ...?
When?	¿Cuándo?
How much is/are ...?	¿Cuánto es/son ...?
How far?	¿Qué distancia hay?
What's that?	¿Qué es eso?
What do you want?	¿Qué desea?
What must I do?	¿Qué debo hacer?
Have you ...?	¿Tiene ...?
Is/are there ...?	¿Hay ...?

Have you seen . . . ?	¿Ha visto . . . ?
Please give me . . .	Haga el favor de darme . . .
I want/should like . . .	Quiero . . .

Useful statements

I like it	Me gusta
I don't like it	No me gusta
I'm not sure	No estoy seguro
I don't know	No sé
I didn't know	No sabía
I think so	Creo que sí
I'm hungry	Tengo hambre
I'm thirsty	Tengo sed
I'm tired	Estoy cansado/a
I'm in a hurry	Tengo prisa
I'm ready	Estoy listo/a
Leave me alone	Por favor déjeme
Just a moment	* Un momento

This way, please	* Por aquí/sígame
Take a seat	* Siéntese
Come in!	* ¡Adelante!
It's cheap/expensive	Es barato/caro
It's too much	Es demasiado
That's all	Es todo
You're right	Tiene razón
You're wrong	No tiene razón
Thank you for your help	Muchas gracias por su ayuda
It's beautiful	Es bonito

Language problems

I'm English/American	Soy inglés/americano (inglesa/ americana)
Do you speak English?	¿Habla inglés?
I don't speak Spanish	No hablo español
I don't understand	No entiendo
Would you say that again, please?	Repita eso, por favor
Please speak slowly	Hable despacio, por favor
What is it called in Spanish?	¿Cómo se dice in español?

Polite phrases

Sorry/excuse me	Perdón
That's all right	Está bien
Not at all/don't mention it	De nada
Don't worry	No se preocupe
It doesn't matter	No importa
I beg your pardon?	¿Qué/¿cómo dice?
Am I disturbing you?	¿(Le) molesto?
I'm sorry to have troubled you	Siento haberle molestado
Good/that's fine	Bien/está muy bien

Greetings and hospitality

Good morning/good day	Buenos días[1]
Good afternoon	Buenas tardes
Good evening/good night	Buenas noches
Hello	¡Hola!/¿qué hay?/adiós
How are you?	¿Cómo está (usted)?

1. *Buenos días* and *buenas tardes* are often abbreviated to *buenas*.

Very well, thank you	Muy bien, gracias
Good-bye	Adiós
See you soon	Hasta luego
May I introduce you to my wife/my husband?	Voy a presentarle a mi mujer/mi marido
Glad to know you	Encantado
What's your name?	¿Cómo se llama?
What's your address/telephone number?	¿Cuál es su dirección/su número de teléfono?
Help yourself	* Sírvase
Would you like a drink/cigarette?	* ¿Quiere beber algo?/¿quiere fumar?/¿fuma?
Can I offer you anything?	* ¿Puede ofrecerle algo?
Thanks for having me	Muchas gracias por su hospitalidad
Thanks for the invitation	Muchas gracias por su invitación
Remember me to ...	Muchos recuerdos a ...
Bon voyage!	¡Buen viaje!
Good luck/all the best	¡Buena suerte!
Where are you staying?	* ¿Dónde está Usted hospedado/hospedada?
Would you like to have dinner/coffee with me?	¿Le gustaría cenar/tomar café conmigo?
Are you doing anything this evening?	¿Tiene Usted algun plan para esta noche?

SIGNS AND PUBLIC NOTICES[1]

Abierto	Open
Agua potable	Drinking water
Ascensor	Lift/elevator
Banco	Bank
Caballeros	Gentlemen
Caja	Cash desk
Cerrado	Closed
Circulen por la derecha	Keep right
Comisaría	Police
Correos	Post office
Entrada	Entrance
Entrada gratuita	Admission free
Guía	Guide
Hay habitaciones	Vacancies/rooms to let
(Hotel) completo	No vacancies
Información	Information
Intérprete	Interpreter
Lavabos[2]	Lavatory
Libre	Vacant/free/unoccupied

1. See also MOTORING (p. 43).
2. There are several ways of expressing 'lavatory' in Spanish. The doors are marked *señoras* (women), *caballeros* or *señores* (men). In stations they are frequently indicated by *retretes*. In cafés and restaurants the normal way to ask for the lavatory is *los servicios, por favor*. Women sometimes ask for *el tocador* (powder room).

Llamar/llamad	Knock/ring
No hay entradas/localidades	House full (cinema, etc.)
No pisar por la hierba	Keep off the grass
No tocar	Do not touch
Ocupado	Engaged/occupied
Particular	Private
Peatones	Pedestrians
Peligro	Danger
Precaución	Caution
Prohibido . . . bajo multa de . . .	Trespassers will be prosecuted
Prohibido el paso	No entry
Retretes	Lavatory
Salida	Exit
Salida de emergencia	Emergency exit
Se alquilar habitaciones	Rooms to let
Señoras	Ladies
Señores	Gentlemen
Se prohibe fumar	No smoking
Se prohibe la entrada	No admission
Se ruega no . . .	You are requested not to . . .
Reservado	Reserved

MONEY

Is there an exchange bureau near here?	¿Hay algún banco cerca donde se pueda cambiar dinero?
Do you cash travellers' cheques?	¿Cambian cheques de viajero?
Where can I cash travellers' cheques?	¿Dónde puedo cambiar cheques de viajero?
I want to change some English/American money	Quiero cambiar dinero inglés/americano
How much do I get for a pound/dollar?	¿A cuánto está la libra/el dólar?
Can you give me some small change?	Déme algo de dinero suelto, por favor
Sign here, please	* Firme aquí, por favor
Go to the cashier	* Vaya al cajero

Currency table[1]

5	pesetas[2] = 3½p		5	pesetas = 9 cents
10	pesetas = 7p		10	pesetas = 17½ cents

1. In Spain banks are open from 9 a.m. to 1.00 p.m. Monday to Saturday.
2. A 5 peseta coin is often called a *duro*.

50 pesetas = 36p	50 pesetas = 86 cents
100 pesetas = 71p	100 pesetas = $1.72
1,000 pesetas = £7.14	1,000 pesetas = $17.24
£1 = 140 pesetas	$1 = 58 pesetas

These rates of exchange are approximate only and subject to variation.

TRAVEL

On arrival

Customs	* Aduana
Passport control	* Control de pasaportes
Your passport, please	* El pasaporte, por favor
May I see your green card ?	* ¿Me permite ver su carta verde ?
Are you together ?	* ¿Viajan juntos ?
I'm travelling alone	Viajo solo
I'm travelling with my wife/ a friend	Viajo con mi esposa/un amigo
I'm here on business/on holiday	Vengo de negocios/de vacaciones
What is your address in Madrid ?	* ¿(Cuál es) su dirección en Madrid ?
How long are you staying here ?	* ¿Cuánto tiempo va a estar usted aquí ?
How much money have you got ?	* ¿Cuánto dinero trae ?
I have . . . pesetas/pounds/ dollars	Tengo . . . pesetas/libras/dólares
Which is your luggage ?	* ¿Cuál es su equipaje ?
Have you anything to declare ?	* ¿Tiene algo que declarar ?
This is my luggage	Éste es mi equipaje
I have only my personal things in it	Sólo llevo mis cosas personales

Open your bag, please	* Abra la maleta, por favor
Can I shut my case now?	¿Puedo cerrar la maleta ya?
May I go through?	¿Puedo pasar ya?/¿puedo irme?
Where is the information bureau, please?	¿Dónde está (la oficina de) Información?
Porter, here is my luggage	Mozo, éste es mi equipaje
What's the price for each piece of luggage?	¿Cuánto cuesta cada bulto?
I shall take this myself	Yo llevo esto
That's not mine	Eso no es mío
Would you call a taxi?	¿Puede llamarme un taxi?
How much do I owe you?	¿Cuánto le debo?

Buying a ticket[1]

Have you a timetable, please?	¿Tiene un horario?
How much is it first class to...?	¿Cuánto cuesta un billete de primera a...?

1. *La RENFE*, the Spanish railway system, has an office in the centre of most large towns. As ticket offices at railway stations only issue tickets shortly before the departure of the train, most people book their tickets and reserve seats in advance at the *RENFE* office.

You can buy a ticket called a *kilométrico* if you intend to travel 3,000 or more kilometres in Spain. There is a substantial discount on the normal price.

A second/third class to ...	Un billete de segunda/ tercera a ...
A return to ...	Un billete de ida y vuelta a ...
How long is this ticket valid ?	¿Cuánto tiempo dura este billete ?
A book of tickets, please[1]	Un taco (de billetes)
Is there a supplementary charge ?	¿Hay que pagar algún suplemento ?

Signs to look for at stations, termini, etc.

Arrivals	Llegadas
Booking office	Despacho de billetes/taquilla
Buses	Autobuses
Connections	Combinación
Departures	Salidas
Enquiries	Información
Exchange	Cambio
Gentlemen	Retretes/caballeros/señores
Ladies	Retretes/señoras

1. This is only available for underground journeys.

Left luggage	Consigna
Lost property	Oficina de objetos perdidos
No smoking	Se prohibe fumar
Refreshments[1]	Cantina/fonda/bar/restaurante
Reservations	Reservas
Suburban lines	Trenes de cercanías/trenes cortos
Taxi rank	Parada de taxis
Tickets	Billetes
Underground	Metro
Waiting room	Sala de espera

By train and underground[2]

Reservations and enquiries

Where's the railway station (main station)?	¿Dónde está la estación de ferrocarril?
Two seats on the 11.15 tomorrow to ...	Dos reservas para mañana en el tren de las once y cuarto para ...

1. In a station the *cantina* serves drinks and snacks; the *fonda* also serves meals and lets rooms.
2. For help in understanding the answers to these and similar questions see TIME (p. 113), NUMBERS (p. 117), DIRECTIONS (p. 41).

I want to reserve a sleeper	Quiero reservar una cama
How much does a couchette cost?	¿Cuánto cuesta una cama litera?
I want to register this luggage through to ...	Quiero facturar este equipaje directamente a ...
What sort of train is it?[1]	¿Qué clase de tren es?
Is there an earlier/later train?	¿Hay un tren antes/más tarde?
Is there a restaurant car on the train?	¿Lleva el tren restaurante?

Changing

Is there a through train to ...?	¿Hay tren directo a ...?
Do I have to change?	¿Hay que hacer transbordo?
Where do I change?	¿Dónde hay que transbordar?
When is there a connexion to ...?	¿Cuándo hay combinación para ir a ...?

Departure

When does the train leave?	¿A qué hora sale el tren?
Which platform does the train to ... leave from?	¿De qué andén sale el tren para ...?
Is this the train for ...?	¿Es éste el tren para ...?

1. The following kinds of train run in Spain: *talgo* and *ter* for which one pays first class fare plus a supplement; *rápido* and *expreso* – ordinary trains; *correo* and *autovía* are slow trains.

Arrival

When does it get to . . . ?	¿A qué hora llega a . . . ?
Does the train stop at . . . ?	¿Para el tren en . . . ?
How long do we stop here ?	¿Cuánto tiempo paramos aquí ?
Is the train late ?	¿Tiene retraso el tren ?
When does the train from . . . get in ?	¿A qué hora llega el tren que viene de . . . ?
At which platform ?	¿En qué andén ?

On the train

We have reserved seats	Tenemos reservas
Is this seat free ?	¿Está este asiento libre ?
This seat is taken	Este asiento está ocupado

By air

Where's the airline office ?	¿Dónde está la oficina de líneas aéreas ?
I'd like to book two seats on Monday's plane to . . .	Quiero reservar dos billetes para el lunes para el avión de . . .
Is there a flight to Valencia on Thursday ?	¿Hay algún vuelo a Valencia los jueves ?

Are there night flights to . . . ?	¿Hay vuelos nocturnos a . . . ?
When does it leave ?	¿A qué hora sale el avión ?
arrive ?	¿A qué hora llega ?
When's the next plane ?	¿A qué hora es el próximo avión ?
Is there a coach to the airport ?	¿Hay autobús al aeropuerto ?
When must I check in ?	¿A qué hora hay que estar en la terminal ?
Please cancel my reservation to . . .	Quiero anular mi reserva para . . .
I'd like to change my reservation to . . .	Quiero cambiar mi reserva para . . .

By ship

Is there a boat from here to . . . ?	¿Hay barco de aquí a . . . ?
How long does the boat take ?	¿Cuánto tiempo tarda ?
How often does the boat leave ?	¿Cada cuánto tiempo sale el barco ?
Where does the boat put in ?	¿En qué puertos toca ?
Does the boat call at . . . ?	¿Toca (el barco) en . . . ?

When does the next boat leave?	¿A qué hora sale el próximo barco?
Can I book a single berth cabin? a first-class/second-class/ luxury class cabin?	¿Puedo reservar un camarote individual?/un camarote de primera/de segunda/de lujo?
How many berths are there in this cabin?	¿Cuántas camas literas hay en este camarote?
When must we go on board?	¿A qué hora hay que estar a bordo?
When do we dock?	¿A qué hora arribamos?
How long do we stay in port?	¿Cúanto tiempo estamos en el puerto?

By bus or coach[1]

Where's the bus station/coach station?	¿Dónde está la estación de autobuses/coches de línea?
Bus stop	* Parada de autobuses
Request stop	* Parada discrecional

1. *La RENFE,* the railway company, also runs coaches between certain towns and tickets can be bought from *RENFE* offices. Privately owned coaches, known a *coches de línea,* ply mainly between villages.

When does the coach leave?	¿A qué hora sale el coche?
When does the coach get to ...?	¿A qué hora llega el coche a ...?
What stops does it make?	¿En qué sitios para?
How long is the journey?	¿Cuánto se tarda?
We want to take a coach tour round the sights	Queremos visitar los sitios de interés en autocar
Is there an excursion to ... tomorrow?	¿Hay alguna excursión a ... mañana?
Does this bus go to the town centre/beach/station?	¿Va este autobús al centro/a la playa/a la estación?
When's the next bus?	¿Cuándo sale el próximo autobús?
How often do the buses run?	¿Cuándo hay autobuses?
Has the last bus gone?	¿Ha salido ya el último autobús?
Do you go near ...?	¿Pasa este autobús cerca de ...?
Where can I get a bus to ...?	¿Dónde puedo tomar el autobús para ...?
Which bus goes to ...?	¿Qué autobús va a ...?
I want to go to ...	Quiero ir a ...
Where do I get off?	¿Dónde tengo que bajarme?
The bus to ... stops over there	* El autobús de ... para allí
number 30 goes to ...	* El treinta va a ...
you must take a number 24	* Tome el veinticuatro

You get off at the next stop | * Bájese en la próxima parada
The buses run every ten minutes/every hour | * Hay autobuses cada diez minutos/cada hora

By taxi

Are you free? | ¿Está libre?
Please take me to the Madrid hotel/the station/this address | Al hotel Madrid por favor/ a la estación/a esta dirección
Can you hurry, I'm late? | Dése prisa, por favor; llego tarde
I want to see the sights/ main streets | Quiero ver los sitios de interés/ las calles principales
Please wait for me here | Espere aquí, por favor
Stop here | Pare aquí
Is it far? | ¿Está lejos?
How much do you charge by the hour/for the day? | ¿Cuánto cobra por hora/todo el día?
How much will you charge to take me to . . . ? | ¿Cuánto costaría ir a . . . ?
How much is it? | ¿Cuánto es?
That's too much | Es demasiado

Directions

Where is . . . ?	¿Dónde está . . . ?
How do I get to . . . ?	¿Por dónde se va a . . . ?
How far is it to . . . ?	¿Qué distancia hay a . . . ?
How many kilometres ?	¿Cuántos kilómetros ?
How do we get on to the motorway to . . . ?	¿Por dónde se sale a la autopista de . . . ?
Which is the best road to . . . ?	¿Cuál es la mejor carretera para . . . ?
Is it a good road ?	¿Es buena la carretera ?
Is there a motorway ?	¿Hay autopista ?
Will we get to . . . by evening ?	¿Llegaremos a . . . antes de anochecer ?
Where are we now ?	¿Dónde estamos ahora ?
Please show me on the map	Indíquemelo en el mapa, por favor
It's that way	* Es por ahí
It isn't far	* No está lejos
Follow this road for 5 kilometres	* Siga esta carretera unos cinco kilómetros
Keep straight on	* Siga adelante/derecho
Turn right at the crossroads	* Tuerza a la derecha en el cruce

Take the second road on the left	* Tome la segunda carretera a la izquierda
Turn right at the traffic-lights	* Tuerza a la derecha en las luces de tráfico
Turn left after the bridge	* Tuerza a la izquierda después del puente
The best road is the . . .	* La mejor carretera es la . . .
Take the . . . and ask again	* Tome la . . . y pregunte nuevamente

MOTORING

Where can I hire a car?	¿Dónde puedo alquilar un coche?
I want to hire a car and a driver/a self-drive car	Quiero alquilar coche con conductor/sin conductor
How much is it to hire it by the hour/day/week?	¿Cuánto cuesta el alquiler por hora/por día/por semana?
Have you a road map?	¿Tiene un mapa de carreteras?
Where is there a car park?	¿Dónde hay un aparcamiento de coches?
Can I park here?	¿Puedo aparcar aquí?
How long can I park here?	¿Por cuánto tiempo puedo aparcar aquí?
May I see your licence, please	* Su carnet, por favor
No parking	* No estacionarse
Keep right	* Circulen por la derecha
Road works ahead	* Obras
Overtaking prohibited	* No pasar
Road blocked	* Carretera obstruida
No entry	* Prohibido el paso
Diversion	* Desviación
One way street	* Dirección única
Steep hill	* Pendiente
Narrow road	* Calle estrecha
Winding road	* Virajes

Speed limit	* Velocidad limitada
Where's the nearest petrol station?	¿Dónde está la gasolinera más próxima?
How far is the next service station?	¿A qué distancia está la próxima estación de servicio
30 litres of petrol, and please check the oil and water	Treinta litros de gasolina y revise el aceite y el agua, por favor
Fill her up please	Llénelo, por favor
How much is petrol a litre?	¿Cuánto cuesta el litro de gasolina?/¿a cuánto el litro?
The oil needs changing	El aceite necesita cambiarse
Check the tyre pressure, please[1]	Compruebe el aire, por favor
Please change the wheel	Cambie la rueda, por favor
This tyre is flat/punctured	Este neumático está desinflado/pinchado
The valve is leaking	La válvula pierde
The radiator is leaking	Gotea el radiador
Please wash the car	Láveme el coche, por favor
Can I leave the car here?	¿Puedo dejar aquí el coche?
What time does the garage close?	¿A qué hora se cierra el garaje

1. See p. 50.

Repairs

Is there an Austin agent here?	¿Hay aquí agencia Austin?
Have you a breakdown service?	¿Hay servicio de reparaciones de emergencia?
Is there a mechanic?	¿Hay un mecánico?
My car's broken down, can you send someone to tow it?	He tenido avería en el coche, ¿puede mandarme un remolcador?
I've lost my car key	He perdido la llave del coche
The battery is flat, it needs charging	La batería está desgastada, necesita cargarse
My car won't start	No arranca el coche
It's not running properly	No marcha bien
The engine is overheating	El motor está demasiado calentado/se recalienta
The engine knocks/is firing badly	El motor detona/funciona mal
It's smoking	Está echando humo
Can you change this faulty plug?	Puede cambiarme esta bujía estropeada?
There's a petrol/oil leak	Pierde gasolina/aceite
There's a smell of petrol/rubber	Hay olor a gasolina/goma

There's a rattle	Se nota un traqueteo
Something is wrong with my car/ the engine/the lights/the clutch/the gearbox/the brakes/ the steering	Hay algo que no va bien en mi coche/el motor/las luces/ el embrague/la caja de cambios/los frenos/la dirección
I've got electrical/mechanical trouble	Se me ha descompuesto el coche: debe ser algo eléctrico/mecánico
The carburettor needs adjusting	El carburador precisa un reglaje
Can you repair it?	¿Pueden arreglarlo?
How long will it take to repair?	¿Cuánto tiempo necesita para arreglarlo?
What will it cost?	¿Cuánto costará?
When will the car be ready?	¿Cuándo estará el coche arreglado?
I need it as soon as possible/in three hours/in the morning	Lo necesito lo antes posible/ dentro des tres horas/mañana por la mañana
It will take two days	* Tardaremos dos días en arreglarlo
We can repair it temporarily	* Se puede arreglar provisionalmente
We haven't the right spares	* No tenemos los repuestos necesarios
We have to send for the spares	* Tenemos que pedir los repuestos
You will need a new ...	* Necesita un (una) ... nuevo (nueva)

Parts of a car and other vocabulary useful in a garage

accelerate	acelerar
accelerator	el acelerador
anti-freeze	el anticongelante
axle	el eje
battery	la batería
bonnet	el capó
boot/trunk	el cofre
brake	el freno
bumper	los parachoques
carburettor	el carburador
choke	el difusor
clutch	el embrague
crank-shaft	el cigüeñal
cylinder	el cilindro
differential gear	el diferencial
dip stick	el indicador de nivel de aceite
distributor	el distribuidor
door	la puerta
doorhandle	la manilla

drive (to)	conducir
driver	el conductor
dynamo	la dínamo
engine	el motor
exhaust	el (tubo de) escape
fan	el ventilador
fanbelt	la correa del ventilador
flat tyre	el neumático desinflado
foglamp	el faro de niebla
fusebox	la caja de fusibles
gasket	la empaquetadura
gears	los cambios (de velocidad)
gear-box	la caja de cambios/de velocidades
gear-lever	la palanca de cambio de velocidad
grease (to)	engrasar
handbrake	el freno de mano
heater	la calefacción
horn	la bocina/el claxon
ignition	el encendido
ignition key	la llave del encendido
indicator	el indicador

jack	el gato
key	la llave
lights – head/side/rear	los faros/las linternas/las luces traseras
mirror	el espejo
numberplate	la (placa de) matrícula
nut	la tuerca
oil	el aceite
petrol	la gasolina
petrol can	el bidón de gasolina
propellor shaft	el árbol de transmisión
piston	el émbolo
plug	la bujía
(oil/water) pump	la bomba (de aceite/agua)
puncture	el pinchazo
radiator	el radiador
reverse	la marcha atrás
seat	el asiento
shock absorber	el amortiguador
silencer	el silenciador
spanner	la llave inglesa
spares	los repuestos
spare wheel	la rueda de repuesto

sparking plug	la bujía
speedometer	el cuentakilómetros
spring	el resorte/el muelle
stall (to)	atascarse
starter	el arranque
steering	la dirección
steering wheel	el volante
tank	el depósito
tappets	los alza-válvulas
transmission	la transmisión
tyre	el neumático
valve	la válvula
wheel	la rueda
window	la ventanilla
windscreen	el parabrisas
windscreen washers	los lavaparabrisas
windscreen wipers	los limpiaparabrisas

Tyre pressure

lb. per sq. in.	kg. per sq. cm.	lb. per sq. in.	kg. per sq. cm.
16	1·1	36	2·5
18	1·3	39	2·7
20	1·4	40	2·8
22	1·5	43	3·0
25	1·7	45	3·1
29	2·0	46	3·2
32	2·3	50	3·5
35	2·5	60	4·2

A rough way to convert lb. per sq. in. to kg. per sq. cm.: multiply by 7 and divide by 100.

ACCOMMODATION[1]

Booking a room

Rooms to let/vacancies	* Hay habitaciones/se alquilan habitaciones
No vacancies	* (Hotel) completo
Have you a room for the night?	¿Tienen habitación para esta noche?
Do you know another good hotel?	¿Puede recomendarme otro hotel bueno?
I've reserved a room; my name is ...	Tengo habitación reservada; mi nombre es ...
I want a single room with a shower	Quiero habitación individual con ducha
We want a room with a double bed and a bathroom	Queremos habitación con cama de matrimonio y baño
Have you a room with twin beds?	¿Tienen habitación de dos camas?
I want a room with a washbasin	Quiero habitación con lavabo
Is there hot and cold water?	¿Hay agua caliente y fría?
I want a room for two or three days/a week/until Friday	Quiero habitación para dos o tres días/una semana/hasta el viernes

1. See also LAUNDRY (p. 89) and RESTAURANT (p. 59).

In addition to privately owned hotels and pensions Spain also has state-run accommodation called *paradores*, *refugios*, and *albergues de carretera*. You are not allowed to stay in an *albergue* for more than 48 hours.

What floor is the room on?	¿En qué piso está la habitación?
Is there a lift/elevator?	¿Hay ascensor?
Have you a room on the first floor?	¿Tienen habitación en el primer piso?
May I see the room?	¿Puedo ver la habitación?
I'll take this room	Me quedo con esta habitación
I don't like this room	No me gusta esta habitación
Have you another one?	¿Tienen otra?
I want a quiet room	Quiero una habitación tranquila
There's too much noise in this room	Hay mucho ruido en esta habitación
I'd like a room with a balcony	Me gustaría una habitación con balcón
Have you a room looking on to the street/the sea?	¿Tienen habitación que dé a la calle/al mar?
We've only a twin-bedded room	* Sólo tenemos habitación de dos camas
This is the only room vacant	* Esta es la única habitación que tenemos
We shall have another room tomorrow	* Tendremos otra habitación mañana
The room is only available tonight	* La habitación sólo está disponible esta noche
How much is the room per night?	¿Cuánto cuesta la habitación por noche?

Have you nothing cheaper?	¿No tienen habitaciones más baratas?
Is the service (and tax) included?	¿Está todo incluído?
Are meals included?	¿Están las comidas incluídas?
How much is the room without meals?	¿Cuánto es sólo la habitación?
How much is full board/half board?	¿Cuánto es la pensión completa/media pensión?
Do you do bed and breakfast?	¿Se puede tener habitación y desayuno?

In your room

I'd like breakfast in my room, please	Quiero el desayuno en mi habitación
Please wake me at 8.30	Llámeme a las ocho y media
There's no ashtray in my room	No hay cenicero en mi habitación
Can I have more hangers, please?	Quisiera más perchas, por favor
Is there a point for an electric razor?	¿Hay enchufe para máquina de afeitar?
What's the voltage?[1]	¿Qué voltaje hay aquí?

1. The most usual type of current in Spain is 127 volts and 50 cycles.

Where is the bathroom?	¿Dónde está el baño?
Where is the lavatory?	¿Dónde están los servicios?
Is there a shower?	¿Tienen ducha?
There are no towels in my room	No hay toallas en mi habitación
There's no soap	No hay jabón
There's no water	No hay agua
There's no plug in my washbasin	El lavabo no tiene tapón
The washbasin is blocked	El lavabo no corre
There's no toilet paper in the lavatory	No hay papel higiénico en el cuarto de baño
The lavatory won't flush	La cadena del cuarto de baño no funciona
May I have another blanket/ another pillow?	Quisiera otra manta/otra almohada, por favor
The sheets on my bed haven't been changed	No han cambiado las sábanas de mi cama
I can't open my window, please open it	No puedo abrir la ventana; haga el favor de abrirla
It's too hot/cold	Hace demasiado calor/frío
Can the heating be turned up/ down?	¿Pueden abrir/cerrar un poco más la calefacción?
Can the heating be turned on/ off?	¿Pueden abrir/cerrar la calefacción?

Is the room air-conditioned?	¿Tiene la habitación aire acondicionado?
The air conditioning doesn't work	El aire acondicionado no funciona
Come in	Adelante/pase
Put it on the table, please	Póngalo en la mesa
I want these shoes cleaned	¿Pueden limpiarme los zapatos?
Could you get this dress/suit cleaned up a bit?	¿Pueden limpiarme un poco este vestido/traje?
I want this suit pressed	¿Pueden plancharme este traje?
When will it be ready?	¿Cuándo estará?
It will be ready tomorrow	* Estará listo mañana

At the reception desk

My key, please	La llave (de mi cuarto), por favor
Are there any letters for me?	¿Tengo (alguna) carta?
Are there any messages for me?	¿Tengo algún recado?
If anyone phones, tell them I'll be back at 4.30	Si alguien llama por teléfono, digan que vuelvo a las cuatro y media
No one telephoned	* No ha telefoneado nadie

There's a lady/gentleman to see you	* Hay una señora/un señor preguntando por usted
Please ask her/him to come up	Que suba a mi habitación, por favor
I'm coming down (at once)	Bajo (en seguida)
Have you any writing paper/envelopes/stamps?	¿Tienen papel de escribir/sobres/sellos?
Please send the chambermaid	La camarera, por favor
I need a guide/interpreter	Necesito un guía/un intérprete
Where is the dining room?	¿Dónde está el comedor?
What time is breakfast/lunch/dinner?	¿A qué hora es el desayuno/la comida/la cena?
Is there a garage?	¿Hay aquí garaje?
Is the hotel open all night?	¿Está el hotel abierto toda la noche?
What time does it close?	¿A qué hora cierra?

Departure

| I am leaving tomorrow | Me voy mañana |
| Can you have my bill ready? | Quiere darme la cuenta, por favor? |

I shall be coming back on . . ., can I book a room for that date ?	Volveré el . . . ¿pueden reservarme habitación para ese día ?
Could you have my luggage brought down ?	¿Pueden bajarme el equipaje ?
Please order a taxi for me at II a.m.	Quiero un taxi para las once
Thank you for a pleasant stay	Muchas gracias por todo

RESTAURANT

Going to a restaurant

Can you suggest a good restaurant/a cheap restaurant/a vegetarian restaurant?	¿Puede recomendarnos un buen restaurante/un restaurante económico/un restaurante vegetariano?
I'd like to book a table for four at 1 p.m.	Quisiera reservar mesa para cuatro para la una
I've reserved a table; my name is . . .	Tengo mesa reservada a nombre de . . .
Have you a table for three?	¿Hay una mesa para tres?
Is there a table free on the terrace?	¿Hay mesa en la terraza?
This way, please	* Por aquí, por favor
We shall have a table free in half an hour	* Habrá mesa dentro de media hora
We don't serve lunch until 1 p.m.[1]	* La comida no empieza hasta la una
We don't serve dinner until 9 p.m.	* No se sirven cenas hasta las nueve
We stop serving at 4 o'clock	* Dejamos de servir a las cuatro
Where is the lavatory?	¿Dónde están los servicios?
It is downstairs	* Están abajo

1. In Spain lunch is usually served from 1 p.m. to 4 p.m.; dinner from 8 p.m. to midnight. Bars and cafés usually stay open until about 2 a.m.

We are in a (great) hurry	Tenemos (mucha) prisa
Do you serve snacks ?[1]	¿Sirven platos combinados/ bocadillos ?
That was a good meal, thank you	La comida estaba muy bien, gracias

Ordering

Waiter/waitress	Camarero/camarera
May I see the menu, please ?	El menú/la carta, por favor
May I see the wine list, please ?	La lista de vinos, por favor
Is there a set menu ?[2]	¿Tienen menú del día/menú turístico ?
What do you recommend ?	¿Qué recomienda ?
Can you tell me what this is ?	¿Haga el favor de decirme que es ésto ?
What is the speciality of the restaurant ?	¿Cuál es la especialidad de la casa ?
What is the speciality of the region ?	¿Cuál es el plato típico de la región ?

1. A *plato combinado* is a main dish served in bars and cafés. It consists of variou
types of meat, vegetables, fish, eggs, etc., in a number of different combinations
Bocadillos are more substantial than English sandwiches, consisting of half a Vienn
loaf filled with meat, omelette, etc.
2. The *cubierto* is the all-in price of a meal, including wine, bread and swee
Service is always included, though it is customary to leave a small tip. There is n
cover charge in Spanish restaurants.

Would you like to try . . . ?	* ¿Quiere probar . . . ?
There's no more . . .	* No quedan . . .
I'd like . . .	Quiero . . .
May I have peas instead of beans ?	¿Pueden ponerme guisantes en vez de judías ?
Is it hot or cold ?	¿Es este plato caliente o frío ?
This isn't what I ordered, I want . . .	Esto no es lo que he pedido, quiero . . .
Without oil/sauce, please	Sin aceite/sin salsa
Some more bread, please	Más pan, por favor
A little more . . .	Un poco más . . .
This is bad	Está malo
This is undercooked	Está poco hecho
This is stale	Está pasado
This is tough	Está duro

Drinks

What will you have to drink ?	* ¿Qué quieren beber ?
A bottle of the local wine, please	Una botella de vino de la tierra
Do you serve wine by the glass ?	¿Sirven vino por vasos ?

Three glasses of beer, please	Tres cervezas, por favor
Do you have draught beer?	¿Tienen cerveza de barril?
Two more beers	Dos cervezas más
I'd like another glass of water, please	Otro vaso de agua, por favor
The same again, please	Lo mismo
Three black coffees and one with milk	Tres cafés solos y uno con leche
I want to see the head waiter/manager	Quiero ver al jefe de comedor/al encargado
May we have an ashtray?	Un cenicero, por favor
Can I have a light, please?	Una cerilla, por favor

Paying

The bill, please	La cuenta
Please check the bill – I don't think it's correct	Revise la cuenta, por favor, creo que no está bien
I didn't have soup	No he tomado sopa
I had chicken, not lamb	Tomé pollo y no cordero
May we have separate bills?	Puede darme la cuenta por separado

Breakfast

A large white coffee/a black coffee, please	Un café con leche doble/un café solo, por favor
would like tea with milk/lemon	Un té con leche (fría)/limón
May we have some sugar, please ?	Azúcar, por favor
A roll and butter	Pan y mantequilla
Toast	Tostadas
More butter, please	Más mantequilla, por favor
Have you some jam ?	¿Tienen mermelada ?
I'd like a soft-boiled/hard-boiled egg	Un huevo pasado por agua/ cocido
Bacon and eggs, please	Beicon y huevo, por favor
What fruit juices have you ?	¿Qué zumos de frutas tienen ?

Restaurant vocabulary

ashtray	el cenicero
bar	el bar
beer	la cerveza

bill	la cuenta
bottle/half bottle	una botella/media botella
bread	el pan
butter	la mantequilla
carafe	la jarra de vino
cigarettes	los cigarrillos/pitillos
cigar	el puro
cloakroom	el guardarropa
coffee	el café
course/dish	el plato
cup	la taza
fork	el tenedor
glass	el vaso
hungry (to be)	tener hambre
jug of water	la jarra de agua
knife	el cuchillo
lemon	el limón
matches	las cerillas
mayonnaise	la mayonesa
menu	el menú
milk	la leche
mustard	la mostaza
napkin	la servilleta

oil	el aceite
pepper	la pimienta
plate	el plato
restaurant	el restaurante
salt	la sal
sandwich	el bocadillo
toasted sandwich	el bocadillo caliente
sauce	la salsa
saucer	el platillo
service	el servicio
snacks	los bocadillos/platos ligeros
spoon	la cuchara
sugar	el azúcar
table	la mesa
table cloth	el mantel
tea	el té
terrace	la terraza
thirsty (to be)	tener sed
tip	la propina
toothpick	el palillo
vegetarian	vegetariano
vinegar	el vinagre
waiter	el camarero

waitress	la camarera
water	el agua
wine	el vino
wine list	la lista de vinos

THE MENU

<table>
<tr><td>

SOPAS

Caldo

Caldo de pollo

Caldo de (rabo de) buey

Gazpacho

Sopa de ajo

Sopa de cebolla

Sopa de fideos

Sopa de gallina

Sopa de mariscos

Sopa de pescado

Sopa de tomate

Sopa de verduras

</td><td>

SOUPS

consommé

chicken consommé

oxtail

cold soup of tomatoes, cucumber, olive oil, garlic, etc.

garlic soup with bread, egg and meat

onion

noodle

chicken

shellfish

fish

tomato

vegetable

</td></tr>
<tr><td>

ENTREMESES

Aceitunas

Alcachofas

Anchoas

Arenques

Boquerones/chanquetes

Caracoles

Ensalada

</td><td>

HORS D'ŒUVRES

olives

artichokes

anchovies

herring

fresh anchovies

snails

salad

</td></tr>
</table>

Espárragos	asparagus
Gambas	prawns
Huevos rellenos	stuffed eggs
Jamón (serrano)	(smoked) ham
Melón	melon
Ostras	oysters
Percebes	goose barnacles
Quisquillas	shrimp
Sardinas	sardines
PESCADOS	**FISH**
Almejas	clams
Anguila	eel
Atún/bonito	fresh tunny
Bacalao	(dried) cod
Bacalao a la Vizcaína	cod stewed with olive oil, pepper onion and tomatoes
Bacalao al Pil-Pil	cod stewed in olive oil to produce a thick, rich sauce
Besugo	sea bream
Calamares	squid
Calamares en su tinta	squid cooked in their own ink
Cangrejo (de mar)	crab
Cangrejo (de río)	crayfish

Centolla	spider crab
Chipirones	baby squid
Gambas	prawns
Langosta	lobster
Lenguado	sole
Mejillones	mussels
Merluza	hake
Pescadillo frito	mixed fried fish
Pez espada	swordfish
Pulpo	octopus
Quisquillas	shrimp
Raya	skate
Rodaballo	turbot
Salmón	salmon
Salmonete	red mullet
Sardinas a la plancha	sardines 'grilled' on the hot plate
Sardinas en escabeche	pickled sardines
Vieiras	scallops
Zarzuela	fish and sea food in a sauce of tomatoes, onions, garlic, bay leaves, olive oil and wine

CARNE	MEAT
Alubias blancas con chorizos	boiled white beans with spicy sausage

Albóndigas	meatballs/rissoles in a tasty sauce
Butifarra con judías	pork sausage with beans
Callos	tripe
Carnero	mutton
Cerdo	pork
Chorizo	sausage made from spiced, cured pig meat
Chuleta	chop
Cochinillo	sucking pig
Cordero asado	roast lamb
Embutidos	sausages
Escalope	escalope
Estofado	stew
Fabada	black pudding and bean stew
Filete	fillet/cutlet
Guisado de ternera	veal stew
Hígado	liver
Jamón	ham
Lacón con grelos	forehams with turnip tops
Lengua	tongue
Lomo	loin
Mollejas	sweetbreads
Pote gallego	hotpot

Puchero cocido	a kind of stew
Riñones	kidneys
Salchichas	sausages
Sesos (huecos)	brains (fried in batter)
Ternera	veal
Tostón	sucking pig
Vaca	beef

AVES Y CAZA	POULTRY AND GAME
Carne de venado	venison
Conejo	rabbit
Faisán	pheasant
Ganso	goose
Liebre	hare
Pato	duck
Pechuga	chicken breast
Perdiz	partridge
Pichones	pigeons
Pollo	chicken

ARROZ	RICE
Pollo con arroz	rice with chicken
Paella valenciana	saffron rice with chicken and seafood

LEGUMBRES Y VERDURAS	VEGETABLES
Ajo	garlic
Alcachofa	artichoke
Alubias	beans
Apio	celery
Berenjena	aubergine/eggplant
Cebolla	onion
Coles	Brussels sprouts
Coliflor	cauliflower
Escarola	endive
Espárragos	asparagus
Espinacas	spinach
Garbanzos	chickpeas
Guisantes	peas
Habas	broad beans
Judías	green beans
Lechuga	lettuce
Lentejas	lentils
Nabo	turnip
Patatas	potatoes
Puerros	leeks
Perejil	parsley
Pimientos	peppers

Rábanos	radishes
Remolacha	beetroot
Repollo	cabbage
Setas	mushrooms
Tomate	tomato
Zanahorias	carrots

HUEVOS	EGGS
Cocidos/duros	hard-boiled
Escalfados	poached
Fritos	fried
Pasados por agua	soft-boiled
Revueltos	scrambled
Tortilla de habas	broad bean omelette
Tortilla de patatas	potato omelette
Tortilla de espárragos	asparagus omelette

POSTRE	DESSERT
Almendrado	macaroon
Buñuelos	fritters
Churros	kind of fried doughnut
Compota	preserved fruit
Flan	crème caramel

Granizado	water ice
Helado	ice cream
Mazapán	marzipan
Merengue	meringue
Natilla	Spanish custard
Pastel/tarta	cake
Turrón	kind of nougat
Yemas	candied egg yolks

FRUTAS Y NUECES	FRUIT AND NUTS
Albaricoque	apricot
Almendra	almond
Avellana	hazel nut
Cereza	cherry
Chirimoya	custard apple
Ciruela	plum
Dátiles	dates
Fresa	strawberry
Higo	fig
Limón	lemon
Manzana	apple
Melocotón	peach
Melón	melon

Membrillo	quince
Naranja	orange
Pasas	raisins
Pera	pear
Piña	pineapple
Plátano	banana
Sandía	water melon
Toronja	grapefruit
Uvas	grapes

BEBIDAS	DRINKS
Agua	water
Agua mineral	mineral water
Anís	anise
Cerveza	beer
Coñac	brandy
Gaseosa	fizzy drink
Ginebra	gin
Horchata	'almond milk'
Leche	milk
Limonada	lemonade
Naranjada	orangeade
Ron	rum

Sangría	red wine mixed with soda water (or champagne), served with ice cubes and slices of lemon and orange
Sidra	cider
Vino	wine
blanco	white
dulce	sweet
espumoso	sparkling
rosé	rosé
seco	dry
tinto	red
Zumo de frutas	fruit juices

COOKING METHODS

a la plancha	'grilled' on the hot plate
a la parilla	grilled
ahumado	smoked
asado	roast
crudo	raw
frito	fried
guisado	braised
medio	medium
muy hecho/asado	well done
poco hecho/asado	rare
relleno	stuffed

SHOPPING

Where to go

Where are the best department stores ?	¿Dónde están los mejores almacenes ?
Which are the best shops ?	¿Cuáles son las mejores tiendas ?
Where is the market ?	¿Dónde está el mercado ?
Is there a market every day ?	¿Hay mercado todos los días ?
Where's the nearest chemist ?	¿Dónde está la farmacia más próxima ?
Can you recommend a hairdresser ?	¿Puede recomendarme una peluquería ?
Where can I buy . . . ?	¿Dónde puedo comprar . . . ?
When are the shops open ?[1]	¿Cuándo abren las tiendas ?

In the shop

Self service	* Autoservicio
Sale (clearance)	* Saldo
Cash desk	* Caja
Shop assistant	El dependiente

1. Shops are open from 9 or 9.30 a.m. to 1.30 p.m., and from 3 or 4 p.m. to 7.30 p.m.

Manager	El encargado/el jefe
Can I help you?	* ¿Qué desea?
I want to buy ...	Quiero comprar ...
Do you sell ...?	¿Venden ustedes ...?
I'm just looking round	Voy a dar una vuelta
I don't want to buy anything now	Por el momento no voy a comprar nada
You'll find them in the ... department	* Eso lo encontrará en el departamento de ...
We've sold out but we'll have more tomorrow	* No tenemos ahora pero tendremos mañana
Shall we send it, or will you take it with you?	* ¿Se lo mandamos, o lo lleva usted?
Please send them to ...	Mándenlo a ...

Choosing

What colour do you want?	* ¿Qué color desea?
I like this one	Me gusta esto
I prefer that one	Prefiero ése
I don't like the colour	No me gusta el color
Have you a green one?	¿Lo tienen en verde?

Do you have different colours?	¿Tienen otros colores?
Have you anything better?	¿Tienen algo mejor?
I'd like another	Quiero otro
What size?[1]	* ¿Qué talla?
It's too big/tight	Es demasiado grande/justo
Have you a larger/smaller one?	¿Tienen más grande/pequeño?
What size is this?	¿Qué talla es ésta?
I want size . . .	Quiero la talla . . .
The English/American size is . . .	La talla inglesa/americana es . . .
My collar size is . . .	Mi medida de cuello es . . .
My chest measurement is . . .	Mi medida de busto es . . .
My waist measurement is . . .	Mi medida de cintura es . . .
What's it made of?	¿De qué es?/¿de qué está hecho?
For how long is it guaranteed?	¿Por cuánto tiempo está garantizado?

Complaints

| I want to see the manager | Quiero hablar con el jefe |
| I bought this yesterday | Compré esto ayer |

1. See Table (pp. 82 and 83) for continental sizes.

It doesn't work	No funciona
This is dirty/stained/torn/ broken/cracked/bad	Está sucio/manchado/roto/ estropeado/rajado/en malas condiciones
Will you change it, please?	¿Pueden cambiármelo?
Will you refund my money?	¿Pueden devolverme el dinero?

Paying

How much is this?	¿Cuánto es esto?
That's 500 pesetas, please	* Son quinientas pesetas
They are 8 pesetas each	* Son ocho pesetas cada uno
It's too expensive	Es demasiado caro
Don't you have anything cheaper?	¿Tienen más barato?
Will you take English/American currency?	¿Aceptan dinero inglés/ americano?
Do you take traveller's cheques?	¿Aceptan cheques de viajero?
Do you give any discount?	¿Hacen descuento?
Please pay the cashier	* Pague en la caja
May I have a receipt, please	Haga el favor de darme recibo
You've given me the wrong change	Creo que el cambio no está bien

Clothes and shoes[1]

I want a hat/sunhat	Quiero un sombrero/sombrero para el sol
I'd like a pair of white cotton gloves/black leather gloves	Quiero un par de guantes blancos de algodón/negros de piel
May I see some dresses, please?	Quiero ver vestidos
I like the one in the window	Me gusta el del escaparate
May I try this?	¿Puedo probarme éste?
That's smart	Éste es muy elegante
It doesn't fit me	No me está bien
I don't like this style	No me gusta este estilo
Ladies'/men's coats, please?	¿Abrigos de señora/de caballeros, por favor?
Where are beach clothes?	¿Dónde están los trajes de playa?
Ladies' hats are on the second floor	* Los sombreros de señora están en el segundo piso
I want a short-/long-sleeved shirt, collar size ...	Quiero una camisa de manga corta/larga, medida de cuello ...
A pair of grey wool socks, please, size ...	Un par de calcetines grises de lana, talla ...

1. For sizes see pp. 82 and 83.

I need a pair of walking shoes/
sandals/black shoes with
small heels

Un par de zapatos cómodos/
sandalias/zapatos negros de
tacón plano

These heels are too high/too low

Este tacón es demasiado alto/
bajo

Clothing sizes

WOMEN'S DRESSES, ETC.

British	32	34	36	38	40	42	44
American	10	12	14	16	18	20	22
Continental	30	32	34	36	38	40	42

MEN'S SUITS

British and American	36	38	40	42	44	46
Continental	46	48	50	52	54	56

MEN'S SHIRTS

British and American	14	14½	15	15½	16	16½	17
Continental	36	37	38	39	41	42	43

STOCKINGS

British and American	8	8½	9	9½	10	10½	11
Continental	0	1	2	3	4	5	6

SOCKS

British and American	9½	10	10½	11	11½
Continental	38-39	39-40	40-41	41-42	42-43

SHOES

British	1	2	3	4	5	6	7	8	9	10	11	12
American	2½	3½	4½	5½	6½	7½	8½	9½	10½	11½	12½	13½
Continental	33	34-5	36	37	38	39-40	41	42	43	44	45	46

This table is only intended as a rough guide since sizes vary from manufacturer to manufacturer.

Chemist[1]

Can you prepare this prescription for me, please ?	¿Pueden hacerme esta receta, por favor ?
Have you a small first-aid kit ?	¿Tienen un pequeño botiquín de urgencia ?

1. See also AT THE DOCTOR'S (p. 107).

A bottle of aspirin, please	Un tubo de aspirinas, por favor
Can you suggest something for indigestion/constipation/ diarrhoea ?	¿Puede recomendarme algo bueno para la indigestión/ el estreñimiento/la colitis ?
I want something for insect bites	Quiero algo para picaduras de insectos
I wan t a mosquito repellant	Quiero algo contra los mosquitos
Can you give me something for sunburn ?	¿Tienen algo para las quemaduras del sol ?
I want some throat lozenges, please	Pastillas para la garganta, por favor

Toilet requisites

A packet of razor blades, please	Un paquete de cuchillas de afeitar, por favor
How much is this after-shave lotion ?	¿Cuánto cuesta esta loción para el afeitado ?
A tube of toothpaste, please	Un tubo de pasta de dientes/ un dentífrico, por favor
A box of paper handkerchiefs, please	Una caja de pañuelos de papel, por favor

I want some eau-de-cologne[1]/ perfume	Un frasco de colonia/colonia a granel/perfume/perfume a granel
May I try it?	¿Puedo probar?
A shampoo for dry/greasy hair, please	Champú para pelo seco/ grasiento, por favor

Photography

I want to buy a camera	Quiero una máquina de fotografiar
Have you a film for this camera?	¿Tienen carretes para esta máquina?
A 120 ... film, please	Un carrete de seis por nueve (6 × 9)
Give me a 35 mm. colour film with 20/36 exposures	Un carrete de color de treinta y cinco milímetros y veinte/ treinta y seis fotos
Would you fit the film in the camera for me, please?	Hace el favor de ponerme el carrete en la máquina
How much is it?	¿Cuánto es?

1. In Spain you can buy 'loose' perfume or eau-de-cologne if you take your own bottle. This is called *perfume/colonia a granel*.

Does the price include processing?	¿Está el revelado incluído?
I'd like this film developed and printed	Quiero revelado y copias de este carrete
Please enlarge this negative	Quiero una ampliación de este negativo
When will it be ready?	¿Cuándo estará?
Will it be done tomorrow?	¿Estará mañana?
Will it be ready by . . .?	¿Puede estar para . . .?
My camera's not working, can you check it/mend it?	Esta máquina no funciona; ¿pueden revisarla/¿pueden arreglármela?
The film is jammed	No pasa el carrete

Food[1]

Give me a kilo/ half a kilo of . . ., please	Un kilo/medio kilo de . . ., por favor
100 grammes of sweets/ chocolates, please	Cien gramos de caramelos/ bombones
A bottle/litre of milk/wine/beer	Una botella/un litro de leche/ vino/cerveza

1. See also RESTAURANT (p. 59) and WEIGHTS AND MEASURES (p. 119).

Is there anything back on the bottle?	¿Devuelven algo por la botella?
I want a jar/tin/packet of ...	Quiero un tarro/una lata/un paquete de ...
Do you sell frozen foods?	¿Venden alimentos congelados?
These pears are very hard	Estas peras están muy duras
Is it fresh?	¿Está fresco?
Are they ripe?	¿Están maduros?
This is bad	Está malo
A loaf of bread, please[1]	Un pan, por favor
How much a kilo/a bottle?	¿Cuánto cuesta el kilo/la botella?

Tobacconist[2]

Do you stock English/American cigarettes?	¿Tienen cigarrillos ingleses/ americanos?
Virginia/dark tobacco	Tabaco rubio/negro
What cigarettes have you?	¿Qué (marcas de) cigarrillos tienen?

1. Spanish bread: *un pan de kilo (medio kilo)* – a loaf weighing 1 kilo ($\frac{1}{2}$ kilo); *un pan de barra* – a French loaf; *bollos/panecillos* – rolls; *un pan de molde* – English loaf.
2. Tobacconists also sell postage stamps. *Estancos* are recognized by a sign bearing the Spanish national colours (red, yellow, red).

A packet of . . ., please	Un paquete de . . .
I want some filter-tip cigarettes/ cigarettes without filter/ mentholated cigarettes	Un paquete de cigarrillos con filtro/sin filtro/mentolados
A box of matches, please	Una caja de cerillas/fósforos
I want to buy a lighter	Quiero comprar un encendedor/ mechero
Do you sell lighter fuel?	¿Tienen gasolina para el encendedor?
I want a gas refill for this lighter	Quiero un recambio de gas para este encendedor

Newspapers, books, writing materials

Do you sell English/American newspapers?	¿Venden periódicos ingleses/ americanos?
Can you get . . . newspaper/ magazine for me?	¿Pueden proporcionarme el diario . . ./la revista . . .?
Where can I get the . . .?	¿Dónde puedo comprar . . .?
I want a map of the city	Quiero un mapa de la ciudad
Is there an entertainment/ amusements guide?	¿Hay una cartelera?
Do you have any English books?	¿Tienen libros ingleses?
Have you any books by . . .?	¿Tienen algún libro de . . .?

I want some coloured postcards/ black and white postcards/ plain postcards

Quiero unas tarjetas postales en color/tarjetas postales en negro/tarjetas postales de correos

Laundry and cleaning

I want to have these things washed/cleaned	Quiero que me laven/limpien esto
These stains won't come out	* Estas manchas no se quitan
It only needs to be pressed	Sólo necesita plancharse
This is torn; can you mend it?	Esto está roto ¿pueden cosérmelo?
Do you do invisible mending?	¿Hacen zurcidos invisibles?
There's a button missing	Me falta un botón
Will you sew on another one, please?	¿Pueden ponerme otro?
When will they be ready?	¿Cuándo estarán?
I need them by this evening/ tomorrow	Lo necesito para esta noche/ para mañana
Call back at 5 o'clock	* Vuelva a las cinco
We can't do it before Thursday	* No podemos hacerlo antes del jueves
It will take three days	* Estará dentro de tres días

Repairs

SHOES

I want these shoes soled with leather/heeled with rubber

Quiero que me pongan mediasuelas de cuero/ punteras de goma

Can you put on new heels?

Pueden ponerse tacones nuevos?

How much do new heels cost?

¿Cuánto cuestan tacones nuevos?

Can you do them while I wait?

¿Pueden arreglármelos en el momento?

When should I pick them up?

¿Cuándo estarán?

WATCH/JEWELLERY

Can you repair this watch?

¿Pueden arreglarme este reloj?

I need a new bracelet/strap

Una cadena/correa nueva, por favor

The fastener is broken

Se ha roto el cierre

The fastener won't work

Se ha estropeado el cierre

The stone is loose

La piedra está suelta

How much will it cost?

¿Cuánto cuesta?

It can't be repaired

* No tiene arreglo

You need a new one

* Necesita un nuevo/una nueva

BARBER AND HAIRDRESSER

May I make an appointment for this morning/tomorrow afternoon?	¿Pueden darme hora para esta mañana/para mañana por la tarde?
What time?	¿A qué hora?
I want my hair cut/trimmed	Quiero cortarme el pelo/cortarme las puntas
Not too short at the sides	No demasiado corto de los lados
I'll have it shorter at the back, please	Más corto por atrás
This is where I have my parting	Aquí la raya
My hair is oily/dry	Tengo el pelo grasiento/seco
I want a shampoo	Quiero que me laven la cabeza
I want my hair washed and set	Quiero que me laven y peinen
Please set it without rollers/on large/small rollers	Sin rulos, por favor/con rulos grandes/pequeños, por favor
I want a colour rinse	Quiero un reflejo
I'd like to see a colour chart	¿Puedo ver colores?
I want a darker/lighter shade	Quiero un tono más oscuro/claro
I want my hair bleached/tinted/permed	Quiero decolorarme/teñirme/una permanente
The water is too cold	El agua está demasiado fría
The dryer is too hot	El secador calienta demasiado

Thank you, I like it very much	Está muy bien
I want a shave/manicure, please	¿Pueden afeitarme/hacerme la manicura, por favor ?

POST OFFICE

Where's the main post office?	¿Dónde está la oficina principal de correos?
Where's the nearest post office?	¿Dónde está la oficina de correos más próxima?
What time does the post office close?	¿A qué hora cierran correos?
Where's the post box?	¿Dónde hay un buzón de correos?

Letters and telegrams[1]

How much is a postcard to England?	¿Qué franqueo llevan las tarjetas postales para Inglaterra?
What's the airmail to the U.S.A.?	¿Qué franqueo llevan las cartas por avión para los Estados Unidos?
How much is it to send a letter surface mail?	¿Qué franqueo llevan las cartas por correo ordinario?
It's inland	Es para España
Give me three 6-peseta and five 1.50-peseta stamps, please	Tres sellos de seis pesetas y cinco de una cincuenta

1. You can buy stamps from a tobacconist's as well as from a post office.

I want to send this letter express	Quiero mandar esta carta urgente
I want to register this letter	Quiero certificar esta carta
Where is the poste restante section?	¿Dónde está la lista de correos?
Are there any letters for me?	¿Hay alguna carta a nombre de . . . ?
What is your name?	* ¿(Cuál es) su nombre, por favor/¿cómo se llama usted?
Have you any means of identification?	* ¿Tiene algo que le identifique?
I want to send an overnight telegram/a reply paid telegram	Quiero mandar un telegrama-carta/un telegrama con respuesta pagada
How much does it cost per word?	¿Cuánto cuesta por palabra?

Telephoning[1]

Where's the nearest phone box?	¿Dónde hay un teléfono público?

1. Telephone boxes are rare, but you can telephone from most cafés and bars. To make a local call you must buy a token (*ficha*); long-distance calls must be made from the *telefónica* (central office). There is no link between the *correos* and the *telefónica*, they are separate services, and post offices do not contain telephones.

I want to make a phone call	Quiero hacer una llamada telefónica
Please give me a token	Una ficha, por favor
Please get me Madrid 2783	Quiero una conferencia con el 2783 de Madrid
I want to telephone to England	Quiero poner una conferencia a Inglaterra
I want to reverse the charges (call collect)	Quiero una conferencia con cobro revertido
I want extension 43	Quiero extensión 43
May I speak to Señor Alvarez?	El señor Alvarez, por favor
Who's speaking?	¿De parte de quién/quién habla?
Hold the line, please	* No se retire
Put the receiver down	* Cuelgue el auricular
He's not here	* No está en casa/aquí
He's at ...	* Está ...
When will he be back?	¿Cuándo volverá?
Will you take a message?	¿Haga el favor de decirle...?
Tell him that Mr X phoned	Dígale que ha llamado el señor X
I'll ring again later	Llamaré más tarde
Please ask him to phone me	Dígale que me llame, por favor
What's your number?	* ¿Cuál es su número?
My number is ...	Mi número es ...

I can't hear you	No le oigo bien
The line is engaged	* Comunican
There's no reply	* No contestan
You have the wrong number	* Tiene el número confundido

SIGHTSEEING[1]

What ought one to see here?	¿Qué hay que ver aquí?
What's this building?	¿Qué edificio es éste?
Where is the old part of the city?	¿Dónde está la parte antigua de la ciudad?
When was it built?	¿Cuándo fué construído?
Who built it?	¿Quién lo construyó?
What's the name of this church?	¿Cómo se llama esta iglesia?
What time is mass at ... church?	¿A qué hora hay misa en la iglesia de ...?
What time is the service?[2]	¿A qué hora es el servicio/el culto?
Is there a Protestant church/ synagogue?	¿Hay aquí iglesia protestante/ sinagoga?
Is this the natural history museum?	¿Es éste el museo de historia natural?
When is the museum open?	¿A qué hora está abierto el museo?
Is it open on Sundays?	¿Está abierto los domingos?
The museum is closed on Mondays	* El museo está cerrado los lunes
Admission free	* Entrada gratuita
How much is it to go in?	¿Cuánto cuesta la entrada?
Have you a ticket?	* ¿Tiene usted entrada?

1. See also BUS AND COACH TRAVEL (p. 38), DIRECTIONS (p. 41).
2. *Servicio* is a service in a Protestant church, *culto* in a Catholic church.

Where do I get tickets?	¿Dónde se sacan las entradas?
Please leave your parcels in the cloakroom	* Dejen los paquetes en el guardarropa
It's over there	* Está por allí
Can I take pictures?	¿Puedo sacar fotografías?
Photographs are prohibited	* Se prohibe hacer fotografías
Follow the guide	* Siga al guía
Does the guide speak English?	¿Habla el guía inglés?
We don't need a guide	No necesitamos guía
Where is the . . . collection/exhibition?	¿Dónde está la colección/exposición de . . .?
Where are the Goyas?	¿Dónde está la sala de Goya?
Where can I get a catalogue?	¿Dónde se compran catálogos?
Where can I get a plan/guide book of the city?	¿Dónde puedo comprar un plano/una guía de la ciudad?
Is this the way to the zoo?	¿Se va por aquí al parque zoológico?
Which bus goes to the castle?	¿Qué autobús va al castillo?
How do I get to the park?	¿Cómo se va al parque?
Can we walk it?	¿Se puede ir andando?

ENTERTAINMENT

What's on at the theatre/cinema?[1]	¿Qué hay en los teatros/cines?
Is there a concert?	¿Hay algún concierto?
I want two seats for tonight	Quiero dos entradas para esta noche
I want to book seats for Thursday	Quiero reservar entradas para el jueves
Are they good seats?	¿Son estas entradas buenas?
Where are these seats?	¿Dónde están estos asientos?
What time does the performance start?	¿A qué hora empieza la función?
What time does it end?	¿A qué hora termina?
A programme, please	Un programa, por favor
Which is the best nightclub?	¿Cuál es la mejor sala de fiestas?
What time is the floorshow?	¿A qué hora es el espectáculo?
Can I have this dance?	¿Quiere bailar?
Is there a jazz club here?	¿Hay alguna sala/algún club de jazz?
Do you have a discotheque here?	¿Tienen discoteca?
What should one wear?	¿Cómo hay que ir vestido?

1. Usually there are two performances daily in theatres and some cinemas. The first (*tarde*) begins at 7.30 or 8 p.m., the second (*noche*) at 10.30 or 11 p.m. Theatres often have three performances on Sundays, starting at 4.30 p.m. In other cinemas the show goes on continuously, starting at about 4.30.

SPORTS AND GAMES

Where is the stadium?	¿Dónde está el estadio?
Are there any seats left in the grandstand?	¿Hay entradas de tribuna?
How much are the cheapest seats?	¿Cúanto cuestan las entradas más baratas?
Are the seats in the sun/shade?	¿Están estos asientos al sol/a la sombra?
We want to go to a football match/the tennis tournament/the bullfight	Queremos ir a un partido de football/al campeonato de tenis/a los toros
Who's playing?	¿Qué equipo juega?
Who's (bull) fighting?	¿Quién torea?
When does it start?	¿A qué hora empieza?
What is the score?	¿Cómo va el marcador?
Who's winning?	¿Quién gana?
Where's the race course?	¿Dónde está el hipódromo?
Which is the favourite?	¿Cuál es el favorito?
Who's the jockey?	¿Quién es el jinete?
100 pesetas to win on .../ each way on ...	Cien pesetas a ganador/a ganador y colocado
What are the odds?	¿A cómo van las apuestas?

THE BULLFIGHT[1]

The bull-ring

LA CORRIDA

la plaza de toros

1. *La novillada* is a corrida with young bulls and inexperienced bullfighters (*novilleros*).

Tickets[1]	entradas
in the sun (cheaper)	de sol
in the shade (more expensive)	de sombra
Ringside (best) seats	barreras
Second-best seats	contrabarreras
Seats directly behind the *contrabarreras*	tendidos
A box	un palco
The gods	la galería
The balcony	el balconcillo
The bullfighter	el torero
Horsemen with lances who weaken the bull	los picadores
The men who place the darts in the bull's shoulder muscles	los banderilleros
The darts	las banderillas
Red and yellow cloak used at the beginning of the *corrida*	la capa/el capote
Small cape used for dangerous passes and preparation for the kill	la muleta
The kill	la estocada
The stabbing at the base of the skull if the bull is not killed immediately	el descabello

1. For a good bullfight tickets cost from 200–700 pesetas.

The ear (the bullfighter may be awarded one or both ears or the tail, dependant upon his performance)	la oreja
The tail	el rabo

ON THE BEACH

Which is the best beach?	¿Cuál es la mejor playa?
Is there a quiet beach near here?	¿Hay por aquí alguna playa tranquila?
Is it far to walk?	¿Se puede ir andando?
Is there a bus to the beach?	¿Hay autobús a la playa?
Is the beach sand or shingle?	¿Es playa de arena o de piedras?
Is the bathing dangerous from this beach/bay?	¿Es peligroso bañarse en esta playa/bahía?
Bathing prohibited	* Prohibido bañarse
It's dangerous	* Hay peligro
Is the tide rising/falling?	¿Está subiendo/bajando la marea?
There's a strong current here	* Aquí hay mucha corriente
You will be out of your depth	* No se hace pie
Are you a strong swimmer?	* ¿Nada bien?
Is it deep?	¿Hay mucha profundidad?
Is the water cold?	¿Está el agua fría?
It's warm	Está caliente
Can one swim in the lake/river?	¿Se puede nadar en el lago/río?
Is there an indoor/outdoor swimming pool?	¿Hay piscina cubierta/al aire libre?
Is it salt or fresh water?	¿Es agua dulce o salada?
Are there showers?	¿Hay duchas?

I want to hire a cabin for the day/morning/two hours

Quiero alquilar una caseta para todo el día/para la mañana/por dos horas

I want to hire a deckchair/sunshade

Quiero alquilar una hamaca/una sombrilla

Can we water ski here?

¿Se puede hacer aquí ski acuático?

Can we hire the equipment?

¿Se puede alquilar el equipo?

Where's the harbour?

¿Dónde está el puerto?

Can we go out in a fishing boat?

¿Se puede salir en barcos de pesca?

We want to go fishing

Queremos ir de pesca

Can I hire a rowing boat/motor boat?

¿Se puede alquilar un barco de remo/una motora?

What does it cost by the hour?

¿Cuánto cuesta por hora?

CAMPING AND WALKING[1]

How long is the walk to the Youth Hostel?	¿Qué distancia hay al Albergue Juvenil?
How far is the next village?	¿A qué distancia está el próximo pueblo?
Is there a footpath to . . . ?	¿Hay camino a . . . ?
Is it possible to go across country?	¿Se puede ir a campo travieso?
Is there a short cut?	¿Hay algún atajo?/¿hay camino más corto?
It's an hour's walk to . . .	* Hay una hora de camino a . . .
Is there a camping site near here?	¿Hay por aquí un camping?
Is this an authorized camp site?	¿Es un camping autorizado?
Is drinking water/are sanitary arrangements/showers provided?	¿Hay agua potable/servicios/duchas?
May we camp here?	¿Se puede acampar aquí?
Can we hire a tent?	¿Podemos alquilar una tienda de campaña?
Can we park our caravan here?	¿Podemos poner aquí nuestro remolque?
Is this drinking water?	¿Se puede beber esta agua?
Where are the shops?	¿Dónde están las tiendas?
Where can I buy paraffin/butane gas?	¿Dónde se puede comprar petróleo/butano?

1. See also DIRECTIONS (p. 41).

May we light a fire?	¿Se puede hacer fuego?
Where do I dispose of rubbish?	¿Dónde puedo tirar las basuras?

AT THE DOCTOR'S

I must see a doctor, can you recommend one?	Quiero que me vea un médico, ¿puede recomendarme alguno?
Please call a doctor	Llame al médico, por favor
I am ill	No estoy bien
I've a pain in my right arm	Me duele el brazo derecho
My wrist hurts	Me duele la muñeca
I think I've sprained/broken my ankle	Creo que me he dislocado/roto el tobillo
I fell down and my back hurts	Me he caído y me duele la espalda
My foot is swollen	Tengo el pie hinchado
I've burned/cut/bruised myself	Me he quemado/cortado/dado un golpe
My stomach is upset	Tengo mal al estómago
I have indigestion	No hago bien la digestión/tengo indigestión
My appetite's gone	No tengo apetito
I think I've got food poisoning	Creo que estoy intoxicado
I can't eat/sleep	No puedo comer/dormir
I am a diabetic	Soy diabético
My nose keeps bleeding	Sangro por la nariz frecuentemente
I have earache	Me duelen los oídos
I have difficulty in breathing	No respiro bien

I feel dizzy	Estoy mareado
I feel sick	Tengo nauseas/ganas de devolver
I keep vomiting	Tengo vómitos
I think I've caught 'flu	Creo que tengo gripe
I've got a cold	Tengo catarro
I've had it since yesterday/for a few hours	Lo tengo desde ayer/desde hace unas horas
You're hurting me	Me hace daño
Must I stay in bed?	¿Tengo que estar en la cama?
Will you call again?	¿Volverá usted?
How much do I owe you?	¿Cuánto le debo?
When can I travel again?	¿Cuándo podré viajar?
I feel better now	Estoy mejor
Where does it hurt?	* ¿Dónde le duele?
Have you a pain here?	* ¿Le duele aquí?
How long have you had the pain?	* ¿Desde cuándo le duele?
Open your mouth	* Abra la boca
Put out your tongue	* Saque la lengua
Breathe in	* Respire fuerte
Breathe out	* Espire
Does that hurt?	* ¿Le duele eso?
A lot?	* ¿Mucho?

A little ?	* ¿Un poco ?
Please lie down	* Échese
I'll give you some pills/medicine	* Voy a darle unas píldoras/una medicina
Take this prescription to the chemist's	* Lleve esta receta a la farmacia
Take this three times a day	* Tome la medicina tres veces al día
I'll give you an injection	* Voy a ponerle una inyección
Roll up your sleeve	* Levántese la manga
I'll put you on a diet	* Voy a ponerle un régimen
Come and see me again in two days' time	* Vuelva dentro de dos días
You must be X-rayed	* Hay que hacerle una radiografía
You must go to hospital	* Tiene usted que ir a un hospital/una clínica
You must stay in bed	* Tiene que estar en la cama

AT THE DENTIST'S

I must see a dentist	Quiero ir al dentista
Can I make an appointment?	¿Pueden darme hora?
As soon as possible	Lo antes posible
I have toothache	Me duelen las muelas
This tooth hurts	Me duele esta muela
I've lost a filling	Se me ha caído un empaste
Can you fill it?	¿Puede empastarme?
Can you do it now?	¿Puede hacérmelo ahora?
Will you take the tooth out?	¿Tiene que sacarme la muela?
Please give me an injection first	Con inyección, por favor
My gums are swollen/keep bleeding	Tengo las encías inflamadas/ me sangran las encías
I've broken my plate, can you repair it?	Se me ha roto la dentadura, ¿me la pueden arreglar?
You're hurting me	Me está haciendo mucho daño
How much do I owe you?	¿Cuánto es, por favor?
When should I come again?	¿Cuándo tengo que volver?
Please rinse your mouth	* Enjuáguese
I will X-ray your teeth	* Tengo que hacerle una radiografía
You have an abscess	* Tiene usted un absceso
The nerve is exposed	* El nervio está al aire
This tooth can't be saved	* Esta muela no se puede salvar

PROBLEMS AND ACCIDENTS

Where's the police station?	¿Dónde está la comisaría?
Call the police	Llame a la policía
Where is the British consulate?	¿Dónde está el consulado inglés?
Please let the consulate know	Comuniquen con el consulado
My bag has been stolen	Me han robado el bolso
I found this in the street	He encontrado esto en la calle
I have lost my luggage/ passport/traveller's cheques	He perdido mi equipaje/ mi pasaporte/mis cheques de viajero
I have missed my train	He perdido el tren
My luggage is on board	Mi equipaje está en el tren
Call a doctor	Llame a un médico
Call an ambulance	Llame una ambulancia
There has been an accident	Ha habido un accidente
We've had an accident	Hemos tenido un accidente
He's badly hurt	Está gravemente herido
He has fainted	Está sin conocimiento
He's losing blood	Está perdiendo sangre
Please get some water/a blanket/ some bandages	(Tráiganos) agua/una manta/ vendas, por favor
I've broken my glasses	Se me han roto las gafas
I can't see	No veo
A child has fallen in the water	Se ha caído al agua un niño

A woman is drowning	Se está ahogando una mujer
May I see your insurance policy ?	* Quiero ver su póliza de seguro
Apply to the insurance company	Diríjase à la compañía de seguros
I want a copy of the police report	Quiero una copia del informe policial

TIME AND DATES

What time is it?	¿Qué hora es?
It's one o'clock	Es la una
2 o'clock	Son las dos
midday	Es mediodía
midnight	medianoche
quarter to ten	Son las diez menos cuarto
quarter past five	las cinco y cuarto
half past four	las cuatro y media
five past eight	las ocho y cinco
twenty to three	las tres menos veinte
twenty-five to seven	las siete menos veinticinco
twenty-five past eight	las ocho y veinticinco
It's early/late	Es temprano/tarde
My watch is slow/fast	Mi reloj está atrasado/ adelantado
My watch has stopped	Se ha parado mi reloj
What time does it start/finish?	¿A qué hora empieza/termina?
Are you staying long?	¿Va a estar mucho tiempo?
I'm staying for two weeks/four days	Estaré dos semanas/cuatro días
I've been here for a week	He estado aquí una semana
We're leaving on January 5th[1]	Nos marchamos el cinco de enero

1. Cardinal numbers are used for dates in Spanish, except for 1st which is *primero*.

We got here on July 27th	Llegamos el veintisiete de julio
What's the date?	¿A cuántos estamos?/¿qué día es hoy?
It's December 9th	A nueve de diciembre/hoy es a nueve
Today	hoy
Yesterday	ayer
Tomorrow	mañana
Day after tomorrow	pasado mañana
Day before yesterday	anteayer
Day	el día
Morning	la mañana
Afternoon	la tarde
Evening	el anocher
Night	la noche
This morning	esta mañana
Yesterday afternoon	ayer por la tarde
Tomorrow night	mañana por la noche
In the morning	por la mañana
In 10 days' time	dentro de diez días
On Tuesday	el martes
On Sundays	los domingos
This week	esta semana
Last month	el mes pasado

Next year	el próximo año/el año que viene
Sunday	domingo
Monday	lunes
Tuesday	martes
Wednesday	miércoles
Thursday	jueves
Friday	viernes
Saturday	sábado
January	enero
February	febrero
March	marzo
April	abril
May	mayo
June	junio
July	julio
August	agosto
September	setiembre
October	octubre
November	noviembre
December	diciembre

PUBLIC HOLIDAYS

1 January	Año nuevo
6 January	Día de Reyes
19 March	Sán José
Good Friday	Viernes santo
Holy Saturday	Sábado de Pasíon
1 May	Fiesta del Trabajo
Ascension Day	Día de la Asención
Corpus Christi	Corpus Cristi
29 June	San Pedro y San Pablo
18 July	Día del Alzamiento (National Holiday)
25 July	Día de Santiago (patron saint of Spain)
15 August	Día de la Asunción
12 October	Fiesta de la Hispanidad
1 November	Todos los Santos
8 December	Immaculada Concepción
25 December	Navidad

Apart from these holidays every town and village celebrates its own holiday which usually coincides with the day of its patron saint.

NUMBERS

CARDINAL

0	cero	21	veintiuno
1	uno/un, una	22	veintidos
2	dos	30	treinta
3	tres	31	treinta y uno
4	cuatro	40	cuarenta
5	cinco	41	cuarenta y uno
6	seis	50	cincuenta
7	siete	51	cincuenta y uno
8	ocho	60	sesenta
9	nueve	61	sesenta y uno
10	diez	70	setenta
11	once	71	setenta y uno
12	doce	80	ochenta
13	trece	81	ochenta y uno
14	catorce	90	noventa
15	quince	91	noventa y uno
16	diez y seis/dieciseis	100	cien/ciento
17	diez y siete/diecisiete	101	ciento uno
18	diez y ocho/dieciocho	200	doscientos
19	diez y nueve/ diecinueve	500	quinientos
20	veinte	700	setecientos

1000	mil	6th	sexto, -a
2000	dos mil	7th	séptimo, -a
1,000,000	un millón	8th	octavo, -a
		9th	noveno, -a
		10th	décimo, -a
ORDINAL		half	medio, -a/la mitad
1st	primero/primer, primera		
2nd	segundo, -a	quarter	un cuarto
3rd	tercero, -a	three quarters	tres cuartos
4th	cuarto, -a	a third	un tercio
5th	quinto, -a	two thirds	dos tercios

Distance: kilometres – miles

km.	miles or km.	miles	km.	miles or km.	miles
1.6	1	0.6	14.5	9	5.6
3.2	2	1.2	16.1	10	6.2
4.8	3	1.9	32.2	20	12.4
6.4	4	2.5	40.2	25	15.3
8	5	3.1	80.5	50	31.1
9.7	6	3.7	160.9	100	62.1
11.3	7	4.4	804.7	500	310.7
12.9	8	5.0			

rough way to convert from miles to km.: divide by 5 and multiply by 8; from km. to miles divide by 8 and multiply by 5.

Length and height:
centimetres – inches

cm.	ins. or cm.	ins.	cm.	ins. or cm.	ins.
2.5	1	0.4	17.8	7	2.8
5.1	2	0.8	20	8	3.2
7.6	3	1.2	22.9	9	3.5
10.2	4	1.6	25.4	10	3.9
12.7	5	2.0	50.8	20	7.9
15.2	6	2.4	127	50	19.7

A rough way to convert from inches to cm.: divide by 2 and multiply by 5; from cm. to inches divide by 5 and multiply by 2.

metres – feet

m.	ft or m.	ft		m.	ft or m.	ft
0·3	1	3·3		2·4	8	26·3
0·6	2	6·6		2·7	9	29·5
0·9	3	9·8		3	10	32·8
1·2	4	13·1		6·1	20	65·6
1·5	5	16·4		15·2	50	164
1·8	6	19·7		30·5	100	328·1
2·1	7	23				

A rough way to convert from ft to m.: divide by 10 and multiply by 3; from m. to ft divide by 3 and multiply by 10.

metres – yards

m.	yds or m.	yds		m.	yds or m.	yds
0·9	1	1·1		7·3	8	8·8
1·8	2	2·2		8·2	9	9·8
2·7	3	3·3		9·1	10	10·9
3·7	4	4·4		18·3	20	21·9

m.	yds or m.	yds		m.	yds or m.	yds
4·6	5	5·5		45·7	50	54·7
5·5	6	6·6		91·4	100	109·4
6·4	7	7·7		457·2	500	546·8

A rough way to convert from yds to m.: subtract 10 per cent from the number of yds; from m. to yds add 10 per cent to the number of metres.

Liquid measures: litres – gallons

litres	galls. or litres	galls.		litres	galls. or litres	galls.
4·6	1	0·2		36·4	8	1·8
9·1	2	0·4		40·9	9	2·0
13·6	3	0·7		45·5	10	2·2
18·2	4	0·9		90·9	20	4·4
22·7	5	1·1		136·4	30	6·6
27·3	6	1·3		181·8	40	8·8
31·8	7	1·5		227·3	50	11

1 pint = 0·6 litre.   1 litre = 1·8 pint.

A rough way to convert from galls. to litres: divide by 2 and multiply by 9; from litres to galls. divide by 9 and multiply by 2.

Weight: kilogrammes – pounds

kg.	lb. or kg.	lb.		kg.	lb. or kg.	lb.
0·5	1	2·2		3·2	7	15·4
0·9	2	4·4		3·6	8	17·6
1·4	3	6·6		4·1	9	19·8
1·8	4	8·8		4·5	10	22·1
2·3	5	11·0		9·1	20	44·1
2·7	6	13·2		22·7	50	110·2

A rough way to convert from lb. to kg.: divide by 11 and multiply by 5; from kg. to lb. divide by 5 and multiply by 11.

grammes – ounces

grammes	oz.	oz.	grammes
100	3·5	2	57·1
250	8·8	4	114·3
500	17·6	8	228·6
1,000 (1 kg.)	35	16 (1 lb.)	457·2

Temperature: centigrade – fahrenheit

centigrade °C	fahrenheit °F
0	32
5	41
10	50

centigrade °C	fahrenheit °F
20	68
30	86
40	104

A rough way to convert from °F to °C: deduct 32 and multiply by $\frac{5}{9}$; from °C to °F multiply by $\frac{9}{5}$ and add 32.

VOCABULARY

A

a, an	un, una	oon, oona
able (to be)	poder	po-dair
about	alrededor de	al-re-de-dor de
above	encima (de)	en-thee-ma
abroad	al extranjero	al es-tran-hair-oh
abscess	el absceso	ab-seso
accept (to)	aceptar	a-thep-tar
accident	el accidente	ak-thee-dente
ache	el dolor	do-lor
acquaintance	el conocido	ko-no-thee-doh
across	a través de	a tra-**bes** de
actor	el actor	ak-tor
actress	la actriz	ak-treeth
add	añadir	anya-deer
address	la dirección	dee-rek-**thyon**
advice	el consejo	kon-say-ho
aeroplane	el avión	ab-**yon**
afraid (to be)	tener miedo	ten-air myay-doh
after	después (de)	des-**pwes**
afternoon	la tarde	tar-de
again	otra vez	otra beth
age	la edad	ay-da

agency	la agencia	ahen-thya
agent	el agente	ahen-te
ago	hace	athe
agree (to)	estar de acuerdo	es-tar de ak-wair-doh
air	el aire	a-ee-re
airbed	el colchón de aire	kol-**chon** de a-ee-re
air-conditioning	el aire acondicionado	a-ee-re akon-dee-thyon-adoh
airline	la línea aérea	**lee**-nay-a a-**ay**-ray-a
airmail	el correo aéreo	ko-ray-oh a-**ay**-ray-oh
airport	el aeropuerto	a-ay-ro-pwer-toh
all	todo	toh-doh
allergy	la alergia	al-air-hee-a
allow (to)	permitir	pair-mee-teer
all right	bueno, bien	bway-no, byen
almost	casi	ka-see
alone	solo	so-lo
along	a lo largo	a lo lar-go
already	ya	ya
alter (to)	modificar	mo-dee-fee-kar
although	aunque	a-oon-ke
always	siempre	sy-em-pre
ambulance	la ambulancia	am-boo-lan-thya

America	los Estados Unidos	es-ta-dos oo-nee-dos
American	americano	amer-ee-ka-no
amuse (to)	divertir	dee-bair-teer
amusing	divertido	dee-bair-tee-doh
anaesthetic	el anestésico	anes-tes-ee-ko
ancient	antiguo	an-tee-gwo
and	y	ee
angry	enojado	eno-hadoh
animal	el animal	anee-mal
ankle	el tobillo	to-bee-llyo
annoy (to)	molestar	mo-les-tar
another	otro	ot-ro
answer	la respuesta	res-pwes-ta
answer (to)	contestar	kon-tes-tar
antique	antiguo	an-tee-gwo
any	alguno	al-goo-no
anyone, someone	alguien	alg-yen
anything, something	algo	al-go
anyway	de todos modos	de toh-dos mo-dos
anywhere, somewhere	en alguna parte	en al-goo-na par-te
apartment	el apartamento	apar-ta-men-toh
apologize (to)	disculpar	dees-kool-par
appendicitis	la apendicitis	apen-dee-thee-tees

appetite	el apetito	ap-e-tee-toh
apple	la manzana	man-tha-na
April	abril *m*	ab-reel
architect	el arquitecto	ar-kee-tek-toh
architecture	la arquitectura	ar-kee-tek-toora
arm	el brazo	bra-tho
around	alrededor de	al-ray-de-dor de
arrange (to)	arreglar	arreg-lar
arrival	la llegada	llye-ga-da
arrive (to)	llegar	llye-gar
art	el arte	ar-te
art gallery	la galería de arte	gal-air-**ee**-a de ar-te
artist	el artista	ar-tees-ta
as	como	ko-mo
as much as	tanto como	tan-toh ko-mo
as soon as	tan pronto como	tan pron-toh ko-mo
as well	también	tam-**byen**
ashtray	el cenicero	then-ee-thair-oh
ask (to)	preguntar	pre-goon-tar
asleep	dormido	dor-mee-doh
aspirin	la aspirina	as-pee-ree-na
at	en	en
at last	al fin	al feen

at once	en seguida	en se-gee-da
atmosphere	el ambiente	am-byen-te
attention	la atención	aten-**thyon**
August	agosto *m*	agos-toh
aunt	la tía	**tee**-a
Australia	Australia	ows-tral-ya
Australian	australiano	ows-tral-ya-no
author	el autor	ow-tor
autumn	el otoño	oton-yo
available	disponible	dees-po-nee-ble
awake	despierto	des-pyair-toh
away	fuera	fwair-a

B

baby	el niño	nee-nyo
bachelor	el soltero	sol-tair-oh
back *returned*	de vuelta	de bwel-ta
back	la espalda	es-pal-da
bad	malo	ma-lo
bag	la bolsa	bol-sa
baker's	la panadería	pa-na-dair-**ee-a**
balcony	el balcón	bal-**kon**
ball *dance*	el baile	ba-ee-le

ball *sport*	la pelota	pe-lo-ta
ballpoint pen	el bolígrafo	bol-ee-gra-fo
banana	el plátano	**pla**-ta-no
band *music*	la orquesta	or-kes-ta
bandage	la venda	ben-da
bank	el banco	ban-ko
bar	el bar	bar
barber's	la peluquería	pel-oo-kair-**ee**-a
basket	la cesta	thes-ta
bath	el baño	ban-yo
bathe (to)	bañar	ban-yar
bathing cap	el gorro de baño	gor-ro de ban-yo
bathing costume	el traje de baño	tra-he de ban-yo
bathing trunks	el bañador	ban-ya-dor
bathroom	el cuarto de baño	kwar-toh de ban-yo
battery	la batería	ba-tair-**ee**-a
bay	la bahía	ba-**ee**-a
be (to)	ser,	sair,
	estar	es-tar
beach	la playa	pla-ya
beard	la barba	bar-ba
beautiful	hermoso	air-mo-so
because	porque	por-ke

bed	la cama	ka-ma
bedroom	el dormitorio	dor-mee-tor-yo
beef	la vaca	ba-ka
beer	la cerveza	thair-bay-tha
before	antes	an-tes
begin (to)	empezar	em-pe-thar
beginning	el principio	preen-thee-pyo
behind	atrás	a-**tras**
believe (to)	creer	kray-air
bell	la campana	kam-pa-na
belong (to)	pertenecer	pair-ten-e-thair
below	abajo	a-ba-ho
belt	el cinturón	thin-toor-**on**
berth	la litera	lee-tair-a
best	el mejor	me-hor
better	mejor	me-hor
between	entre	en-tre
bicycle	la bicicleta	bee-thee-klay-**ta**
big	grande	gran-de
bill	la cuenta	kwen-ta
bird	el pájaro	**pa**-ha-ro
birthday	el cumpleaños	koom-ple-an-yos
bite (to)	morder	mor-dair

black	negro	ne-gro
blanket	la manta	man-ta
bleach (to)	decolorar	de-ko-lor-ar
bleed (to)	sangrar	san-grar
blister	la ampolla	am-poll-ya
blood	la sangre	san-gre
blouse	la blusa	bloo-sa
blue	azul	a-thool
(on) board	a bordo	a bor-doh
boarding house	la pensión	pen-sy-on
boat	el barco	bar-ko
body	el cuerpo	kwair-po
bone	el hueso	way-so
book	el libro	lee-bro
book (to)	reservar	res-air-bar
booking office	el despacho de billetes	des-pacho de bee-llye-tes
bookshop	la librería	lee-brair-ee-a
borrow (to)	pedir prestado	pe-deer pres-ta-doh
both	ambos	am-bos
bottle	la botella	bo-te-llya
bottle opener	el abrebotellas	abre-bo-te-llyas
bottom	el fondo	fon-doh

owl	el tazón	ta-**thon**
ox *container*	la caja	ka-ha
ox *theatre*	el palco	pal-ko
ox office	la taquilla	ta-kee-llya
oy	el muchacho	moo-cha-cho
racelet	la pulsera	pool-sair-a
races	los tirantes	tee-ran-tes
rain	el seso	se-so
rake (to)	frenar	fre-nar
randy	el coñac	kon-yak
rassière	el sostén	sos-**ten**
read	el pan	pan
reak (to)	romper	rom-pair
reakfast	el desayuno	des-a-yoo-no
reathe (to)	respirar	res-pee-rar
ridge	el puente	pwen-te
right *colour*	vivo	bee-bo
ring (to)	traer	tra-air
British	británico	bree-**tan**-ee-ko
roken	roto	ro-toh
brooch	el broche	bro-che
brother	el hermano	air-ma-no
brown	marrón	mar-**ron**

bruise	la contusión	kon-too-sy-**on**
bruise (to)	magullar	ma-goo-llyar
brush	el cepillo	the-pee-llyo
brush (to)	cepillar	the-pee-llyar
bucket	el cubo	koo-bo
build (to)	construir	kon-strweer
building	el edificio	edee-fee-thyo
bullfight	la corrida de toros	kor-ree-da de to-ros
bullring	la plaza de toros	pla-tha de to-ros
buoy	la boya	bo-ya
burn (to)	quemar	ke-mar
burst (to)	reventar	re-ben-tar
bus	el autobús	ow-toh-**boos**
bus stop	la parada	pa-ra-da
business	el negocio	ne-go-thyo
busy	ocupado	okoo-pa-do
but	pero	pe-ro
butcher's	la carnicería	kar-nee-thair-**ee**-a
butter	la mantequilla	man-te-kee-llya
button	el botón	bo-**ton**
buy (to)	comprar	kom-prar
by	por	por

C

cabin	el camarote	ka-ma-ro-te
cable	el telegrama	tele-grama
café	el café	ka-**fe**
cake	el pastel	pas-tel
call (to) *summon, name*	llamar	llya-mar
(telephone) call	la llamada (telefónica)	llya-mada tele-**fon**-ee-ka
call (to) *visit*	visitar	bee-see-tar
camera	la máquina fotográfica	**ma**-kee-na foto-**gra**-fee-ka
camp (to)	acampar	akam-par
camp site	el camping	kam-peeng
can (to be able)	poder	po-dair
can *tin*	la lata	la-ta
Canada	Canadá *m*	ka-na-**da**
Canadian	canadiense	ka-na-dyen-se
cancel (to)	anular	a-noo-lar
canoe	la canoa	ka-no-a
cap	la gorra	gor-ra
capital city	la capital	ka-pee-tal
car	el coche	ko-che
car licence	la documentación	do-koo-men-ta-thy**on**

car park	el estacionamiento	es-ta-thyon-a-myen-toh
carafe	la garrafa	gar-ra-fa
caravan	el remolque	re-mol-ke
care	el cuidado	kwee-da-do
careful	cuidadoso	kwee-da-do-so
carry (to)	llevar	llye-bar
cash (to)	cambiar	kam-byar
cashier	el cajero	ka-hair-oh
casino	el casino	ka-see-no
castle	el castillo	kas-tee-llyo
cat	el gato	ga-toh
catalogue	el catálogo	ka-**ta**-lo-go
catch (to)	coger	ko-hair
cathedral	la catedral	ka-te-dral
catholic	católico	ka-**toh**-lee-ko
cave	la cueva	kwe-ba
centre	el centro	then-tro
century	el siglo	see-glo
ceremony	la ceremonia	the-re-mon-ya
certain	seguro	se-goo-ro
chair	la silla	see-llya
chambermaid	la camarera	ka-ma-rair-a

(small) change	el dinero suelto	dee-nair-oh swel-toh
change (to)	cambiar	kam-byar
charge	la tarifa	ta-ree-fa
charge (to)	cobrar	kob-rar
cheap	barato	ba-ra-toh
check (to)	examinar	eg-sam-ee-nar
cheek	la mejilla	may-heel-lya
cheese	el queso	ke-so
chemist's	la farmacia	far-ma-thee-a
cheque	el cheque	che-ke
chest	el pecho	pe-cho
chicken	el pollo	po-llyo
child	el niño	nee-nyo
chill	el enfriamiento	en-free-a-myen-toh
chin	la barbilla	bar-bee-llya
china	la porcelana	por-the-lana
chiropodist	el pedicuro	pe-dee-koo-ro
chocolate	el chocolate	cho-ko-la-te
chop	la chuleta	choo-le-ta
Christmas	la Navidad	na-bee-da
church	la iglesia	ee-gle-sya
cider	la sidra	see-dra
cigar	el puro	poo-roh

cigarette	el pitillo,	pee-tee-llyo,
	el cigarrillo	the-gar-ree-llyo
cigarette case	la pitillera	pee-tee-llyair-a
cigarette lighter	el encendedor	en-then-de-dor
cinema	el cine	thee-ne
circle *theatre*	el anfiteatro	an-fee-te-atro
circus	el circo	theer-ko
city	la ciudad	thyoo-da
class	la clase	kla-se
clean (to)	limpiar	leem-pyar
clean	limpio	leem-pyo
cliff	el acantilado	acan-tee-la-doh
cloakroom	el guardarropa	gwar-dar-ropa
clock	el reloj	re-loh
close (to)	cerrar	ther-rar
closed	cerrado	ther-ra-do
cloth	la tela	te-la
clothes	los trajes	tra-hes
coach	el coche	ko-che
coast	la costa	kos-ta
coat	el abrigo	abree-go
coffee	el café	ka-**fe**
coin	la moneda	mo-ne-da

cold	frío	free-oh
cold *med*	el catarro	ka-tar-ro
cold cream	la crema para la cara	kre-ma para la kara
collar	el cuello	kwe-llyo
collar stud	el pasador	pa-sa-dor
colour	el color	ko-lor
colour film	el carrete de color	kar-re-te de ko-lor
colour rinse	el reflejo	re-fle-ho
comb	el peine	pe-ee-ne
come (to)	venir	be-neer
come in	¡adelante!	ade-lan-te
comfortable	cómodo	**ko**-mo-do
compartment *train*	el departamento	de-par-ta-men-toh
complain (to)	quejarse	ke-har-se
complete	completo	kom-ple-toh
concert	el concierto	kon-thyair-toh
conductor *bus*	el cobrador	ko-bra-dor
conductor *orchestra*	el director de orquesta	dee-rek-tor de or-kes-ta
congratulations	¡felicidades!	fe-lee-thee-da-des
connexion *train, etc.*	la combinación	kom-bee-na-**thyon**
constipation	el estreñimiento	es-tren-yee-myen-toh
consul	el cónsul	**kon**-sool

consulate	el consulado	kon-sool-adoh
contain (to)	contener	kon-ten-air
convenient	conveniente	kon-ben-yen-te
convent	el convento	kon-ben-toh
conversation	la conversación	kon-bair-sa-**thyon**
cook	el cocinero	ko-thee-nair-oh
cook (to)	cocer	ko-thair
cooked	cocido	ko-thee-doh
cool	fresco	fres-ko
copper *metal*	el cobre	ko-bre
cork	el corcho	kor-cho
corkscrew	el sacacorchos	sa-ka-kor-chos
corner	la esquina	es-kee-na
correct	correcto	kor-rek-to
corridor	el pasillo	pa-see-llyo
cosmetics	las pinturas	peen-too-ras
cost	el precio	pre-thyo
cost (to)	costar	kos-tar
cotton	el algodón	al-go-**don**
cotton wool	el algodón	al-go-**don**
couchette	la litera	lee-tair-a
cough	la tos	tos
count (to)	contar	kon-tar

country *nation*	el país	pa-ees
countryside	el campo	kam-po
course *dish*	el plato	pla-toh
cousin	el primo	pree-mo
cramp	el calambre	ka-lam-bre
cream	la crema	kre-ma
cross	la cruz	krooth
cross (to)	atravesar	atra-be-sar
crossroads	el cruce de carreteras	kroo-the de kar-re-tair-as
cufflinks	los gemelos	he-me-los
cup	la taza	ta-tha
cupboard	el armario	ar-ma-ryo
cure (to)	curar	koo-rar
curl (to)	rizar	ree-thar
current	la corriente	kor-ryen-te
curtain	la cortina	kor-tee-na
custard	las natillas	na-tee-llyas
customs	la aduana	a-dwan-a
customs officer	el oficial de aduana	off-ee-thyal de a-dwan-a
cut	la cortadura	kor-ta-doo-ra
cut (to)	cortar	kor-tar
cutlet	la costilla	kos-tee-llya

D

daily	diario	dee-ar-yo
damaged	dañado	dan-ya-doh
damp	húmedo	**oo**-me-doh
dance	el baile	ba-ee-le
dance (to)	bailar	ba-ee-lar
danger	el peligro	pe-lee-gro
dangerous	peligroso	pe-lee-gro-so
dark	oscuro	os-koo-ro
date	la fecha	fe-cha
daughter	la hija	ee-ha
day	el día	**dee**-a
dead	muerto	mwair-toh
deaf	sordo	sor-doh
dear	caro	ka-ro
December	diciembre *m*	dee-thyem-bre
deck	la cubierta	koo-byair-ta
deckchair	la hamaca	a-ma-ka
declare (to)	declarar	de-kla-rar
deep	profundo	pro-foon-doh
delay	el retraso	re-tra-so
delicatessen	la mantequería	man-te-kair-**ee**-a
deliver (to)	entregar	en-tre-gar

delivery	el reparto	re-par-toh
demi-pension	la media pensión	me-dya pen-**syon**
dentist	el dentista	den-tees-ta
deodorant	el desodorante	de-so-dor-an-te
depart (to)	salir	sa-leer
department	el departamento	de-par-ta-men-toh
department store	el almacén	alma-**then**
departure	la salida	sa-lee-da
dessert	el postre	pos-tre
detour	la desviación	des-bya-**thyon**
develop *film*	revelar	re-be-lar
diabetic	diabético	dya-**be**-tee-ko
diamond	el brillante	bree-llyan-te
diarrhoea	la colitis	ko-lee-tees
dictionary	el diccionario	deek-thyo-nar-yo
diet	la dieta	dye-ta
diet (to)	estar a dieta	es-tar a dye-ta
different	diferente	dee-fair-en-te
difficult	difícil	dee-**fee**-theel
dine (to)	cenar	the-nar
dining room	el comedor	ko-me-dor
dinner	la cena	the-na
direction	la dirección	dee-rek-**thyon**

dirty	sucio	soo-thyo
discothèque	la discoteca	dees-ko-te-ka
dish	el plato	pla-toh
disinfectant	el desinfectante	de-seen-fek-tan-te
distance	la distancia	dees-tan-thya
disturb (to)	molestar	mo-les-tar
dive (to)	tirarse de cabeza	tee-rar-se de ka-be-tha
diving board	el trampolín	tram-po-**leen**
divorced	divorciado	dee-bor-thya-doh
dizzy	mareado	ma-re-ado
do (to)	hacer	a-thair
dock (to)	atracar	atra-kar
doctor	el médico	**me**-dee-ko
dog	el perro	per-ro
doll	la muñeca	moon-ye-ka
dollar	el dólar	**do**-lar
door	la puerta	pwair-ta
double	doble	do-ble
double bed	la cama de matrimonio	ka-ma de mat-ree-mo-nyo
double room	la habitación de matrimonio	abee-ta-**thyon** de mat-ree-mo-nyo
down (stairs)	abajo	a-ba-ho
dozen	la docena	do-the-na

drawer	el cajón	ka-**hon**
dress	el vestido	bes-tee-doh
dressing gown	la bata	ba-ta
dressmaker	la modista	mo-dees-ta
drink (to)	beber	be-bair
drinking water	el agua potable	ag-wa po-ta-ble
drive (to)	conducir	kon-doo-theer
driver	el conductor	kon-dook-tor
driving licence	el carnet de conducir	kar-nay de kon-doo-theer
dry (to)	secar	se-kar
dry cleaning	la limpieza en seco	leem-pye-tha en se-ko
duck	el pato	pa-toh
during	mientras	myen-tras

E

each	cada	ka-da
ear	el oído	o-ee-doh
earache	el dolor de oídos	do-lor de o-ee-dos
early	temprano	tem-pra-no
earrings	los pendientes	pen-dyen-tes
east	el este	es-te
Easter	la Pascua	pas-kwa

easy	fácil	**fa**-theel
eat (to)	comer	ko-mair
egg	el huevo	way-bo
elastic	el elástico	e-**las**-tee-ko
elbow	el codo	ko-do
electric light bulb	la bujía eléctrica	boo-**hee**-a el-**ek**-tree-ka
elevator	el ascensor	asen-sor
embassy	la embajada	em-ba-ha-da
emergency exit	la salida de emergencia	sa-lee-da de em-air-hen-thya
empty	vacío	ba-**thee**-oh
end	el fin	feen
engine	la máquina	**ma**-kee-na
England	Inglaterra f	een-gla-ter-ra
English	inglés	een-**gles**
enlargement	la ampliación	amp-lya-thy**on**
enough	bastante	bas-tan-te
enquiries	la información	een-for-ma-thy**on**
entrance	la entrada	en-tra-da
envelope	el sobre	so-bre
equipment	el equipo	e-kee-po
Europe	Europa f	oy-ro-pa
evening	la tarde	tar-de

every	cada	ka-da
everybody	todos	toh-dos
everything	todo	toh-doh
everywhere	en todas partes	en toh-das par-tes
example	el ejemplo	e-hem-plo
except	excepto	es-ep-toh
excess	el exceso	es-es-oh
exchange (bureau)	la casa de cambio	ka-sa de kam-byo
exchange rate	el cambio	kam-byo
excursion	la excursión	es-koor-**syon**
exhibition	la exposición	es-po-see-**thyon**
exit	la salida	sa-lee-da
expect (to)	esperar	es-pair-ar
expensive	caro	ka-ro
express	urgente	oor-hen-te
express train	el rápido	**ra**-pee-doh
eye	el ojo	o-ho

F

face	la cara	ka-ra
factory	la fábrica	**fab**-ree-ka
faint (to)	desmayarse	des-ma-yar-se
fair *fête*	la feria	fe-rya

fair *blonde*	rubio	roo-byo
false teeth	los dientes postizos	dyen-tes pos-tee-thos
fall (to)	caer	ka-air
family	la familia	fa-mee-lya
far	lejos	le-hos
fare	el billete	bee-llye-te
farm	la finca	feen-ka
farther	más lejos	mas le-hos
fashion	la moda	mo-da
fast	rápido	**ra**-pee-doh
fat	gordo	gor-doh
father	el padre	pa-dre
fault	la culpa	kool-pa
February	febrero *m*	feb-rair-oh
feel (to)	sentir	sen-teer
fetch (to)	buscar	boos-kar
fever	la fiebre	fyeb-re
few	pocos	po-kos
field	el campo	kam-po
fig	el higo	ee-go
fill (to)	llenar	llye-nar
filling *tooth*	el empaste	em-pas-te
film *camera*	el carrete	kar-re-te

film *cinema*	la película	pe-**lee**-koo-la
find (to)	hallar	a-llyar
fine	la multa	mool-ta
finger	el dedo	de-doh
finish (to)	acabar	a-ka-bar
finished	acabado	a-ka-ba-doh
fire	el fuego	fwe-go
first	primero	pree-mair-oh
first class	la primera (clase)	pree-mair-a kla-se
fish	el pescado	pes-ka-doh
fish (to)	pescar	pes-kar
fisherman	el pescador	pes-ka-dor
fishmonger's	la pescadería	pes-ka-dair-**ee**-a
fit (to)	sentar	sen-tar
flag	la bandera	ban-dair-a
flat *level*	llano	llya-no
flat	el apartamento	apar-ta-men-toh
flight	el vuelo	bwe-loh
flint *lighter*	la piedra	pye-dra
flood	la inundación	ee-noon-da-**thyon**
floor	el piso	pee-so
floor show	el espectáculo	es-pek-**ta**-koo-lo
florist's	la tienda de flores	tyen-da de flor-es

flower	la flor	flor
fly	la mosca	mos-ka
fly (to)	volar	bo-lar
follow (to)	seguir	se-geer
food	la comida	ko-mee-da
food poisoning	la intoxicación	een-tok-see-ka-**thyon**
foot	el pie	pee-ay
football	el fútbol	**foot**-bol
footpath	el camino	ka-mee-no
for	por, para	por, pa-ra
forehead	la frente	fren-te
forest	la selva	sel-ba
forget (to)	olvidar	ol-bee-dar
fork	el tenedor	te-ne-dor
forward	adelante	ade-lan-te
fracture	la fractura	frak-too-ra
fragile	frágil	**fra**-heel
France	Francia *f*	fran-thya
free	libre	lee-bre
French	francés	fran-**thes**
fresh	fresco	fres-ko
fresh water	el agua dulce	ag-wa dool-the
Friday	viernes *m*	byair-nes

fried	frito	free-toh
friend	el amigo	amee-go
from	de, desde	de, des-de
(in) front	frente	fren-te
frontier	la frontera	fron-tair-a
frozen	congelado	kon-hel-ado
fruit	la fruta	froo-ta
fruiterer's	la frutería	froo-tair-ee-a
fruit juice	el zumo de fruta	thoo-mo de froo-ta
full	lleno	llye-no
full board	la pensión completa	pen-**syon** kom-ple-ta
funny	cómico	**ko**-mee-ko
fur	la piel	pyel

G

gallery	la galería	ga-lair-ee-a
gamble (to)	jugar	hoo-gar
game	el juego	hwe-go
garage	el garaje	ga-ra-he
garden	el jardín	har-**deen**
garlic	el ajo	a-ho
gate	la entrada	en-tra-da
gentlemen	caballeros	ka-ba-llye-ros

gentlemen	señores	sen-yor-es
German	alemán	a-le-**man**
Germany	Alemania *f*	a-le-man-ya
get (to)	obtener	ob-te-nair
get off (to)	bajarse	ba-har-se
get on (to)	subirse	soo-beer-se
gift	el regalo	re-ga-lo
girdle	la faja, tubular	fa-ha, too-boo-lar
girl	la muchacha	moo-cha-cha
give (to)	dar	dar
glad	contento	kon-ten-toh
glass	el vaso	ba-so
glasses	las gafas	ga-fas
gloves	los guantes	gwan-tes
go (to)	ir	eer
God	Dios	dyos
gold	el oro	o-ro
good	bueno	bwe-no
good afternoon/ evening	buenas tardes	bwe-nas tar-des
good-bye	adiós	ad-**yos**
good day/morning	buenos días	bwe-nos **dee**-as
good night	buenas noches	bwe-nas no-ches

government	el gobierno	go-byair-no
granddaughter	la nieta	nye-ta
grandfather	el abuelo	abwe-lo
grandmother	la abuela	abwe-la
grandson	el nieto	nye-to
grape	la uva	oo-ba
grapefruit	la toronja	to-ron-ha
grass	la hierba	yer-ba
grateful	agradecido	ag-ra-de-thee-doh
great	grande	gran-de
green	verde	bair-de
greengrocer's	la frutería	froo-tair-ee-a
	la verdulería	bair-doo-lair-ee-a
grey	gris	grees
grocer's	la especiería	es-peth-yair-ee-a
groceries	comestibles	ko-mes-tee-bles
guarantee	la garantía	ga-ran-tee-a
guest	el huésped	wes-ped
guide	el guía	gee-a
guide book	la guía	gee-a
gum	la encía	en-thee-a

H

hair	el pelo	pe-lo
hair brush	el cepillo para el pelo	the-pee-llyo para el pe-lo
haircut	el corte de pelo	kor-te de pe-lo
hairdresser's	la peluquería	pe-loo-kair-**ee**-a
hairgrips, hairpins	las horquillas	or-kee-llyas
half	medio	me-dyo
half fare	el medio billete	me-dyo bee-llye-te
ham	el jamón	ha-**mon**
hand	la mano	ma-no
handbag	el bolso	bol-so
handkerchief	el pañuelo	pan-ywe-lo
hanger	la percha	pair-cha
happen (to)	suceder	soo-the-dair
happy	feliz	fe-leeth
harbour	el puerto	pwair-toh
hard	duro	doo-ro
hat	el sombrero	som-brair-oh
have (to)	tener	te-nair
have to (to)	deber	de-bair
hay-fever	la fiebre de heno	fye-bre de e-no
he	él	el

head	la cabeza	ka-be-tha
headache	el dolor de cabeza	do-lor de ka-be-tha
head waiter	el jefe de comedor	hefe de ko-me-dor
health	la salud	sa-lood
hear (to)	oír	o-**eer**
heart	el corazón	ko-ra-**thon**
heat	el calor	ka-lor
heating	la calefacción	ka-le-fak-**thyon**
heavy	pesado	pe-sa-doh
heel *foot*	el talón	ta-**lon**
heel *shoe*	el tacón	ta-**kon**
help	la ayuda	a-yoo-da
help (to)	ayudar	a-yoo-dar
her *adj.*	su	soo
here	aquí	a-**kee**
high	alto	al-toh
hill	la colina	ko-lee-na
hip	la cadera	ka-dair-a
hire (to)	alquilar	al-kee-lar
his	su	soo
hitch hike (to)	hacer auto-stop	a-thair ow-toh-stop
holiday	el día de fiesta	**dee**-a de fyes-ta
holidays	las vacaciones	ba-ka-thyo-nes

(at) home	en casa	en ka-sa
honey	la miel	my-el
hors d'œuvres	los entremeses	en-tre-mes-es
horse	el caballo	ka-ba-llyo
horse races	las carreras de caballos	kar-rair-as de ka-ba-llyos
hospital	el hospital	os-pee-tal
hot	caliente	kal-yen-te
hotel	el hotel	o-tel
hotel keeper	el gerente	he-ren-te
hot water bottle	la bolsa (de agua caliente)	bol-sa
hour	la hora	or-a
house	la casa	ka-sa
how ?	¿cómo ?	ko-mo
how much, many ?	¿cuánto ?, ¿cuántos ?	kwan-to(s)
hungry (to be)	tener hambre	te-nair am-bre
hurry (to)	darse prisa	dar-se pree-sa
hurt (to)	doler	do-lair
husband	el marido	ma-ree-doh

I

I	yo	yo
ice	el hielo	ye-lo

ice cream	el helado	e-lado
if	si	see
ill	enfermo	en-fair-mo
illness	la enfermedad	en-fair-me-da
immediately	inmediatamente	een-me-dya-ta-men-te
important	importante	eem-por-tan-te
in	en	en
include	incluir	een-kloo-eer
included	incluído	een-kloo-ee-do
inconvenient	incómodo	een-ko-mo-do
incorrect	incorrecto	een-kor-rek-to
indigestion	la indigestión	een-dee-hes-**tyon**
infection	la infección	een-fek-**thyon**
influenza	la gripe	gree-pe
information	la información	een-for-ma-**thyon**
injection	la inyección	een-yek-**thyon**
ink	la tinta	teen-ta
inn	la posada	po-sa-da
insect	el insecto	een-sek-toh
insect bite	la picadura de insecto	pee-ka-doo-ra de een-sek-toh
inside	dentro (de)	den-troh
insomnia	el insomnio	een-som-nyo

insurance	el seguro	se-goo-ro
insure (to)	asegurar	ase-goo-rar
interesting	interesante	een-tair-es-an-te
interpreter	el intérprete	een-**tair**-pre-te
into	en, dentro (de)	en, den-tro
introduce (to)	presentar	pre-sen-tar
invitation	la invitación	een-bee-ta-**thyon**
invite (to)	invitar	een-bee-tar
Ireland	Irlanda *f*	eer-lan-da
Irish	irlandés	eer-lan-**des**
iron (to)	planchar	plan-char
island	la isla	ees-la
it	él, ella	el, ellya
Italian	italiano	ee-tal-ya-no
Italy	Italia *f*	ee-tal-ya

J

jacket	la chaqueta	cha-ke-ta
jam	la mermelada	mair-me-la-da
January	enero *m*	e-nair-oh
jar	el tarro	tar-ro
jaw	la mandíbula	man-**dee**-boo-la
jellyfish	la medusa	me-doo-sa

jeweller's	la joyería	hoy-air-**ee**-a
jewellery	las joyas	hoy-as
journey	el viaje	bya-he
jug	jarra	har-ra
juice	el zumo	thoo-mo
July	julio *m*	hoo-lyo
June	junio *m*	hoo-nyo
jumper	el jersey	hair-say

K

keep (to)	guardar	gwar-dar
key	la llave	llya-be
kidney	el riñón	reen-**yon**
kind	la clase	kla-se
king	el rey	ray
kitchen	la cocina	ko-thee-na
knee	la rodilla	ro-dee-llya
knickers, briefs	las bragas	bra-gas
knife	el cuchillo	koo-chee-llyo
know (to) *fact*	saber	sa-bair
know (to) *person*	conocer	ko-no-thair

L

label	la etiqueta	etee-ke-ta

lace	el encaje	en-ka-he
ladies	señoras	sen-yor-as
lamb	el cordero	kor-dair-oh
lamp	la lámpara	**lam**-pa-ra
landlord	el propietario	pro-pye-tar-yo
lane	el camino	ka-mee-no
language	el idioma	ee-dyo-ma
large	grande	gran-de
last	último	**ool**-tee-mo
late	tarde	tar-de
laugh (to)	reír	re-eer
laundry	la lavandería	la-ban-dair-**ee**-a
lavatory	los servicios	sair-bee-thyos
lavatory paper	el papel higiénico	pa-pel ee-**hyen**-ee-ko
law	la ley	lay
laxative	el laxante	lak-san-te
lead (to)	conducir	kon-doo-theer
learn (to)	aprender	a-pren-dair
leather	la piel, el cuero	pyel, kwair-oh
leave (to) *abandon*	dejar	de-har
leave (to) *go out*	salir	sa-leer
left *opp. right*	izquierdo	eeth-kyair-doh
left luggage	la consigna	kon-sig-na

leg	la pierna	pyair-na
lemon	el limón	lee-**mon**
lemonade	la limonada	lee-mo-na-da
lend (to)	prestar	pres-tar
length	el largo	lar-go
less	menos	me-nos
let (to) *rent*	alquilar	al-kee-lar
let *allow*	dejar	de-har
letter	la carta	kar-ta
lettuce	la lechuga	le-choo-ga
library	la biblioteca	bee-blyo-te-ka
licence	la licencia	lee-then-thya
life	la vida	bee-da
lift	el ascensor	asen-sor
light *colour*	claro	kla-ro
light	la luz	looth
light meter	el fotómetro	fo-**to**-me-tro
lighter	el encendedor	en-then-de-dor
lighter fuel	la gasolina	ga-so-lee-na
lighthouse	el faro	fa-ro
like (to)	querer	ke-rer
linen	el hilo	ee-lo
lip	el labio	la-byo

lipstick	la barra de labios	bar-ra de la-byos
listen	escuchar	es-koo-char
little	poco	po-ko
live (to)	vivir	bee-beer
liver	el hígado	ee-ga-doh
loaf	el pan	pan
local	local	lo-kal
lock (to)	cerrar con llave	ther-rar kon llya-be
long	largo	lar-go
look (to)	mirar	mee-rar
look (to) *seem*	parecer	pa-re-thair
look for (to)	buscar	boos-kar
lorry	el camión	ka-**myon**
lose (to)	perder	pair-dair
lost property office	la oficina de objetos perdidos	off-ee-thee-na de ob-he-tos pair-dee-dos
loud	ruidoso	rwee-doh-so
love (to)	querer	ke-rair
lovely	hermoso	air-mo-so
low	bajo	ba-ho
luggage	el equipaje	e-kee-pa-he
(piece of) luggage	el bulto	bool-toh
lung	el pulmón	pool-**mon**

M

magazine	la revista	re-bees-ta
maid	la doncella	don-the-llya
mail	el correo	kor-ray-oh
main street	la calle principal	ka-llye preen-thee-pal
make (to)	hacer	a-thair
make-up	el maquillaje	ma-kee-llya-he
man	el hombre	om-bre
manager	el director	dee-rek-tor
manicure	la manicura	ma-nee-koo-ra
many	muchos	moo-chos
map	el mapa	ma-pa
March	marzo *m*	mar-tho
market	el mercado	mair-ka-do
marmalade	la mermelada	mer-me-la-da
married	casado	ka-sa-do
Mass	la misa	mee-sa
match	la cerilla	the-ree-llya
match *sport*	el partido	par-tee-doh
material	la tela	te-la
mattress	el colchón	kol-**chon**
May	mayo *m*	ma-yo
meal	la comida	ko-mee-da

measurements	las medidas	me-dee-das
meat	la carne	kar-ne
medicine	la medicina	me-dee-thee-na
meet (to)	encontrar	en-kon-trar
melon	el melón	me-**lon**
mend (to)	reparar	re-pa-rar
menu	el menú	me-**noo**
message	el recado	re-ka-doh
metal	el metal	me-tal
midday	el mediodía	me-dyo-**dee-a**
middle	el medio	me-dyo
midnight	la media noche	me-dya no-che
milk	la leche	le-che
mineral water	el agua mineral *f*	ag-wa mee-nair-al
minute	el minuto	mee-noo-toh
mirror	el espejo	es-pe-ho
Miss	la señorita	sen-yor-ee-ta
miss (to) *train, etc.*	perder	pair-dair
mistake	la equivocación	ekee-bo-ka-**thyon**
modern	moderno	mo-dair-no
moment	el momento	mo-men-toh
Monday	lunes *m*	loo-nes
money	el dinero	dee-nair-oh

money order	el giro postal	hee-ro pos-tal
month	el mes	mes
more	más	mas
morning	la mañana	ma-nya-na
mosquito	el mosquito	mos-kee-toh
mother	la madre	ma-dre
motor	el motor	mo-tor
motor boat	la motora	mo-tor-a
motor cycle	la motocicleta	mo-toh-thee-kle-ta
motor racing	las carreras de coches	kar-rair-as de ko-ches
motorway	la autopista	ow-toh-pees-ta
mountain	la montaña	mon-tan-ya
mouth	la boca	bo-ka
Mr	el señor	sen-yor
Mrs	la señora	sen-yor-a
much	mucho	moo-cho
muscle	el músculo	**moos**-koo-lo
museum	el museo	moo-se-oh
mushroom	la seta	se-ta
music	la música	**moo**-see-ka
must (to have to)	deber	de-bair
mustard	la mostaza	mos-ta-tha

| mutton | el carnero | kar-nair-oh |
| my | mi | mee |

N

nail *finger*	la uña	oon-ya
nailbrush	el cepillo de uñas	the-pee-llyo de oon-yas
nailfile	la lima	lee-ma
name	el nombre	nom-bre
napkin	la servilleta	sair-bee-llye-ta
nappy	el pañal	pan-yal
narrow	estrecho	es-tre-cho
nausea	la náusea	na-oo-se-a
near	cerca	thair-ka
necessary	necesario	ne-the-sa-ryo
neck	el cuello	kwe-llyo
necklace	el collar	ko-llyar
need (to)	necesitar	ne-the-see-tar
needle	la aguja	ag-oo-ha
nerve	el nervio	nair-byo
never	nunca	noon-ka
new	nuevo	nwe-bo
news	las noticias	no-tee-thyas

newsagent	el quiosco (de periódicos)	kyos-ko
newspaper	el periódico	pe-**ryo**-dee-ko
next	próximo	**pro**-see-mo
nice	bonito	bo-nee-toh
night	la noche	no-che
nightclub	la sala de fiestas	sa-la de fyes-tas
nightdress	el camisón	ka-mee-**son**
no	no	no
nobody	nadie	na-dye
noisy	ruidoso	rwee-doh-so
none	ninguno	neen-goo-no
north	el norte	nor-te
nose	la nariz	na-reeth
not	no	no
note *money*	el billete	bee-llye-te
notebook	el cuaderno de notas	kwa-dair-no de no-tas
nothing	nada	na-da
notice	el aviso	a-bee-so
novel	la novela	no-be-la
November	noviembre *m*	no-byem-bre
number	el número	**noo**-mair-oh
nurse	la enfermera	en-fair-mair-a

nut	la nuez	noo-eth
nylon	el nilón	nee-**lon**

O

occupied	ocupado	okoo-pa-doh
October	octubre *m*	ok-too-bre
odd *strange*	raro	ra-ro
of	de	de
office	la oficina	off-ee-thee-na
official	oficial	off-ee-thyal
often	frecuentemente	fre-kwen-te-men-te
oil	el aceite	a-thay-te
oily	grasiento	gra-syen-toh
ointment	el ungüento	oon-goo-en-toh
old	viejo	bye-ho
olive	la aceituna	a-thay-too-na
on	en, sobre	en, so-bre
once	una vez	oona beth
only	solamente	so-la-men-te
open (to)	abrir	ab-reer
open *p p*	abierto	ab-yair-toh
opera	la ópera	**o**-pair-a
operation	la operación	o-pair-a-**thyon**
opposite	enfrente (de)	en-fren-te

optician	el óptico	**op**-tee-ko
or	o	o
orange	la naranja	na-ran-ha
orchestra	la orquesta	or-kes-ta
order (to)	pedir	pe-deer
ordinary	ordinario	or-dee-na-**ryo**
other	otro	o-tro
our, ours	nuestro	nwes-tro
out, outside	fuera, afuera	fwe-ra, a-fwe-ra
over	sobre	so-bre
overcoat	el abrigo	ab-ree-go
over there	por allí	por a-**llyi**
owe (to)	deber	de-ber
owner	el propietario	pro-pye-ta-ryo

P

packet	el paquete	pa-ke-te
page	la página	**pa**-hee-na
paid	pagado	pa-ga-doh
pain	el dolor	do-lor
paint (to)	pintar	peen-tar
painting	la pintura	peen-too-ra
pair	el par	par

palace	el palacio	pa-la-thyo
pale	pálido	**pa**-lee-doh
paper	el papel	pa-pel
paraffin	el petróleo	pe-**tro**-lee-oh
parcel	el paquete	pa-ke-te
park (to)	aparcar	apar-kar
park	el parque	par-ke
part	la parte	par-te
parting *hair*	la raya	ra-ya
pass (to)	pasar	pa-sar
passenger	el viajero	bya-hair-oh
passport	el pasaporte	pa-sa-por-te
path	la senda	sen-da
patient	el enfermo	en-fair-mo
pay (to)	pagar	pa-gar
pea	el guisante	gee-san-te
peach	el melocotón	me-lo-ko-**ton**
pear	la pera	pe-ra
pearl	la perla	per-la
pebble	la piedra	pyed-ra
pedestrian	el peatón	pe-a-**ton**
pen	la pluma	ploo-ma
pencil	el lápiz	**la**-peeth

penknife	la navaja	na-ba-ha
people	la gente	hen-te
pepper	la pimienta	pee-myen-ta
performance	la representación	re-pre-sen-ta-**thyon**
perfume	el perfume	pair-foo-me
perhaps	quizás	kee-**thas**
perm	la permanente	pair-ma-nen-te
permit	el permiso	pair-mee-so
permit (to)	permitir	pair-mee-teer
person	la persona	pair-so-na
personal	personal	pair-so-nal
petrol	la gasolina	ga-so-lee-na
petrol can	el bidón (de gasolina)	bee-**don**
petrol station	la gasolinera	ga-so-lee-ne-ra
photograph	la fotografía	fo-toh-gra-**fee**-a
photographer	el fotógrafo	fo-**toh**-gra-fo
piano	el piano	pya-no
picnic	la merienda	me-ryen-da
picnic (to)	ir de merienda	eer de me-ryen-da
piece	la pieza	pye-tha
pillow	la almohada	al-mo-ada
pin	el alfiler	al-fee-lair

(safety) pin	el imperdible	eem-pair-dee-ble
pineapple	la piña	peen-ya
pink	rosa	ro-sa
pipe	la pipa	pee-pa
place	el sitio	see-tyo
plan	el plano	pla-no
(sticking) plaster	el esparadrapo	es-pa-ra-dra-po
plastic	el plástico	**plas**-tee-ko
plate	el plato	pla-toh
platform	el andén	an-**den**
play (to)	jugar	hoo-gar
play	la obra de teatro	ob-ra de te-a-tro
player	el jugador	hoo-ga-dor
please	por favor	por fa-bor
plug *bath*	el tapón	ta-**pon**
plug *electric*	el enchufe	en-choo-fe
plum	la ciruela	theer-we-la
pocket	el bolsillo	bol-see-llyo
point	la punta	poon-ta
poisonous	venenoso	be-ne-no-so
policeman	el agente de policía	ahen-te de po-lee-**thee**-a
police station	la comisaría	ko-mee-sa-**ree**-a

poor	pobre	po-bre
popular	popular	po-poo-lar
pork	el cerdo	thair-doh
port	el puerto	pwair-toh
porter	el mozo	mo-tho
possible	posible	po-see-ble
post (to)	echar al correo	e-char al kor-ray-oh
post box	el buzón	boo-**thon**
postcard	la (tarjeta) postal	tar-hay-ta pos-tal
postman	el cartero	kar-tair-oh
post office	(la oficina de) correos	kor-ray-os
poste restante	lista de correos	lees-ta de kor-ray-os
potato	la patata	pa-ta-ta
pound	la libra	lee-bra
powder *cosmetic*	los polvos	pol-bos
prefer (to)	preferir	pre-fair-eer
prepare (to)	preparar	pre-pa-rar
prescription	la receta	re-the-ta
present *gift*	el regalo	re-ga-lo
press (to)	planchar	plan-char
pretty	bonito	bo-nee-toh
price	el precio	pre-thyo
private	particular	par-tee-koo-lar

problem	el problema	pro-ble-ma
profession	la profesión	pro-fe-**syon**
programme	el programa	pro-gra-ma
promise (to)	prometer	pro-me-tair
pull (to)	tirar	tee-rar
pure	puro	poo-ro
purse	el monedero	mo-ne-dair-oh
push (to)	empujar	em-poo-har
put (to)	poner	po-nair
pyjamas	el pijama	pee-ha-ma

Q

quality	la calidad	ka-lee-da
quantity	la cantidad	kan-tee-da
quarter	el cuarto	kwar-toh
queen	la reina	re-ee-na
question	la pregunta	pre-goon-ta
quick	rápido	**ra**-pee-doh
quiet	tranquilo	tran-kee-lo

R

race	la carrera	kar-re-ra
racecourse	el hipódromo	ee-**po**-dro-mo

radiator	el radiador	ra-dya-dor
radio	la radio	ra-dyo
railway	el ferrocarril	fer-ro-kar-ril
rain	la lluvia	llyoo-bya
(it is) raining	llueve	llyoo-e-be
raincoat	el impermeable	eem-pair-me-a-ble
rangefinder	el telémetro	te-le-me-tro
rare *unusual*	raro	ra-ro
raw	crudo	kroo-doh
razor	la navaja de afeitar	na-ba-ha de a-fay-tar
razor blades	las cuchillas de afeitar	koo-chee-llyas de a-fay-tar
read (to)	leer	lay-er
ready	listo	lees-toh
real	verdadero	bair-da-dair-oh
really	verdaderamente	bair-da-dair-a-men-te
reason	la razón	ra-**thon**
receipt	el recibo	re-thee-bo
receive (to)	recibir	re-thee-beer
recent	reciente	re-thyen-te
recommend (to)	recomendar	re-ko-men-dar
record	el disco	dees-ko
red	rojo	ro-ho

refreshment room	la cantina,	kan-tee-na,
	la fonda	fon-da
register (to)	certificar	thair-tee-fee-kar
registered mail	el correo certificado	kor-ray-oh thair-tee-fee-ka-doh
remember (to)	acordarse	akor-dar-se
rent (to)	alquilar	al-kee-lar
repair (to)	arreglar	ar-reg-lar
repeat (to)	repetir	re-pe-teer
reply (to)	contestar	kon-tes-tar
reply paid	respuesta pagada	res-pwes-ta pa-ga-da
reservation	la reserva	re-sair-ba
reserve (to)	reservar	re-sair-bar
reserved	reservado	re-sair-ba-doh
restaurant	el restaurante	res-tow-ran-te
restaurant car	el coche restaurante	ko-che res-tow-ran-te
return (to)	volver	bol-bair
rib	la costilla	kos-tee-llya
ribbon	la cinta	theen-ta
rice	el arroz	ar-roth
right *opp. left*	derecho	de-re-cho
ring	el anillo	anee-llyo
river	el río	**ree**-oh

road	la carretera	kar-re-tair-a
roasted	asado	a-sa-doh
rock	la roca	ro-ka
roll *bread*	el panecillo	pan-e-thee-llyo
rollers *hair*	los rulos	roo-los
room	la habitación	abee-ta-**thyon**
rope	la soga	so-ga
round	redondo	re-don-do
rowing boat	la barca	bar-ka
rubber	la goma	go-ma
rubbish	la basura	ba-soo-ra
run (to)	correr	kor-rair
Russia	Rusia *f*	roo-sya
Russian	ruso	roo-so

S

safe	seguro	se-goo-ro
salad	la ensalada	en-sa-la-da
salesgirl	la vendedora	ben-de-doh-ra
salesman	el vendedor	ben-de-dor
salt	la sal	sal
salt water	el agua salada *f*	ag-wa sa-la-da
same	mismo	mees-mo

sand	la arena	a-re-na
sandals	las sandalias	san-da-lyas
sandwich	el bocadillo	bo-ka-dee-llyo
sanitary towels	las compresas (higiénicas)	kom-pre-sas ee-**hyen**-ee-kas
Saturday	sábado *m*	**sa**-ba-doh
sauce	la salsa	sal-sa
saucer	el platillo	pla-tee-llyo
sausage	la salchicha	sal-chee-cha
say (to)	decir	de-theer
scald (to)	quemarse	ke-mar-se
scarf	la bufanda	boo-fan-da
scent	el perfume	pair-foo-me
school	la escuela	es-kwe-la
scissors	las tijeras	tee-hair-as
Scotland	Escocia *f*	es-ko-thya
Scottish	escocés	es-ko-**thes**
sculpture	la escultura	es-kool-too-ra
sea	el mar	mar
sea food	los mariscos	ma-rees-kos
seasick	mareado	ma-re-adoh
season	la temporada	tem-po-ra-da
seat	el asiento	a-syen-toh

second	segundo	se-goon-doh
second class	la segunda (clase)	se-goon-da kla-se
sedative	el sedante	se-dan-te
see (to)	ver	bair
seem (to)	parecer	pa-re-thair
self service	servicio automático	sair-bee-thyo ow-toh-**ma**-tee-ko
sell (to)	vender	ben-dair
send (to)	mandar	man-dar
separate	separado	se-pa-ra-doh
September	setiembre *m*	se-tyem-bre
serious	serio	sair-yo
serve (to)	servir	sair-beer
service	el servicio	sair-bee-thyo
service *church: R.C.*	el culto	kool-toh
Prot.	el servicio	sair-bee-thyo
set (to) *hair*	el peinado	pey-na-doh
several	varios	bar-yos
sew (to)	coser	ko-sair
shade *colour*	el matiz	ma-teeth
shade *sun*	la sombra	som-bra
shallow	poco profundo	po-ko pro-foon-doh
shampoo	el champú	cham-**poo**
shape	la forma	for-ma

share (to)	repartir	re-par-teer
sharp	agudo	agoo-doh
shave (to)	afeitar	a-fay-tar
shaving brush	la brocha de afeitar	bro-cha de a-fay-tar
shaving cream	la crema de afeitar	kre-ma de a-fay-tar
she	ella	ellya
sheet	la sábana	**sa**-ba-na
shell	la concha	kon-cha
sherry	el jerez	hair-eth
shine (to)	brillar	bree-llyar
shingle *beach*	el guijarro	gee-har-ro
ship	el barco	bar-ko
shipping line	la línea marítima	**lee**-ne-a ma-**ree**-tee-ma
shirt	la camisa	ka-mee-sa
shoelaces	los cordones de zapatos	kor-doh-nes de tha-pa-tos
shoes	los zapatos	tha-pa-tos
shoe shop	la zapatería	tha-pa-tair-**ee-a**
shop	la tienda	tyen-da
short	corto	kor-toh
shorts	los pantalones cortos	pan-ta-lo-nes kor-tos
shoulder	el hombro	om-bro
show	el espectáculo	es-pek-**ta**-koo-lo

show (to)	mostrar	mos-trar
shower	la ducha	doo-cha
shut (to)	cerrar	ther-rar
shut *p p*	cerrado	ther-ra-doh
sick	enfermo	en-fair-mo
side	el lado	la-doh
sights	los lugares interesantes	loo-gar-es een-tair-es-antes
silk	la seda	se-da
silver	la plata	pla-ta
simple	sencillo	sen-thee-llyo
since	desde	des-de
single	solo	so-lo
single room	la habitación individual	abee-ta-**thyon** een-dee-bee-dwal
sister	la hermana	air-ma-na
sit, sit down (to)	sentarse	sen-tar-se
size	el tamaño	ta-man-yo
skid (to)	patinar	pa-tee-nar
sky	el cielo	thye-lo
sleep (to)	dormir	dor-meer
sleeper	la cama	ka-ma
sleeping bag	el saco de dormir	sa-ko de dor-meer
sleeve	la manga	man-ga

slice	la porción	por-**thyon**
slip	la combinación	kom-bee-na-**thyon**
slippers	las zapatillas	tha-pa-tee-llyas
slow	lento	len-toh
small	pequeño	pe-ken-yo
smart	elegante	ele-gan-te
smell (to)	oler	o-lair
smoke (to)	fumar	foo-mar
(no) smoking	prohibido fumar	pro-ee-bee-do foo-mar
snack	el bocadillo	bo-ka-dee-llyo
snow	la nieve	nye-be
(it is) snowing	nieva	nye-ba
so	así	a-see
soap	el jabón	ha-**bon**
soap powder	el jabón en polvo	ha-**bon** en pol-bo
socks	los calcetines	kal-the-tee-nes
soda water	(el agua de) soda *f*	(ag-wa de) so-da
sold	vendido	ben-dee-doh
sole *fish*	el lenguado	len-gwa-doh
sole *shoe*	la suela	swe-la
some	algunos	al-goo-nos
somebody	alguien	alg-yen
something	algo	al-go

sometimes	algunas veces	al-goo-nas be-thes
somewhere	en algún sitio	en al-**goon** see-tyo
son	el hijo	ee-ho
song	la canción	kan-**thyon**
soon	pronto	pron-toh
sore throat	el dolor de garganta	do-lor de gar-gan-ta
sorry	perdón	pair-**don**
sort	la clase	kla-se
soup	la sopa	so-pa
sour	agrio	ag-ree-oh
south	el sur	soor
souvenir	el recuerdo	re-kwer-doh
Spain	España *f*	es-pan-ya
Spanish	español	es-pan-yol
speak (to)	hablar	ab-lar
speciality	la especialidad	es-pe-thya-lee-da
speed	la velocidad	be-lo-thee-da
speed limit	la velocidad limitada	be-lo-thee-da lee-mee-ta-da
spend (to)	gastar	gas-tar
spine	el espinazo	es-pee-na-tho
spoon	la cuchara	koo-cha-ra
sports	los deportes	de-por-tes

spot *stain*	la mancha	man-cha
sprain	la dislocación	dees-lo-ka-**thyon**
sprain (to)	dislocar	dees-lo-kar
spring	la primavera	pree-ma-bair-a
square	la plaza	pla-tha
stage	el escenario	es-then-ar-yo
stain	la mancha	man-cha
stained	manchado	man-cha-do
stairs	la escalera	es-ka-lair-a
stalls *theatre*	la butaca	boo-ta-ka
stamp	el sello	se-llyo
stand (to)	estar de pie	es-tar de pye
start (to)	empezar	em-pe-thar
station	la estación	es-ta-**thyon**
stationer's	la papelería	pa-pe-le-**ree**-a
statue	la estatua	es-ta-too-a
stay (to)	quedarse	ke-dar-se
steak	el bistec	bees-tek
steward	el mozo	mo-tho
stewardess	la camarera	ka-ma-re-ra
still	todavía	to-da-**bee**-a
sting	el aguijón	ag-ee-**hon**
	la picadura	pee-ka-doo-ra

stockings	las medias	me-dyas
stolen	robado	ro-ba-doh
stomach	el estómago	es-**toh**-ma-go
stomach-ache	el dolor de estómago	do-lor de es-**toh**-ma-**go**
stone	la piedra	pye-dra
stop (to)	parar	pa-rar
store	la tienda	tyen-da
stove	el infiernillo	een-fyair-nee-llyo
straight	derecho	de-re-cho
straight on	todo seguido	toh-doh se-gee-doh
strange	extraño	es-tran-yo
strap	la correa	kor-ray-a
strawberry	la fresa	fre-sa
stream	el arroyo	ar-roy-oh
street	la calle	ka-llye
string	la cuerda	kwair-da
strong	fuerte	fwair-te
student	el estudiante	es-too-dyan-te
style	el estilo	es-tee-loh
suburb	el suburbio	soo-boor-byo
subway	el paso subterráneo	pa-so soob-tair-**ran**-yo
suede	el ante	an-te
sugar	el azúcar	a-**thoo**-kar

suit	el traje (de chaqueta)	tra-he
suitcase	la maleta	ma-le-ta
summer	el verano	bair-ra-no
sun	el sol	sol
sunbathe (to)	tomar el sol	to-mar el sol
sunburn	la quemadura de sol	ke-ma-doo-ra de sol
Sunday	domingo *m*	doh-meen-go
sunglasses	las gafas de sol	ga-fas de sol
sunhat	el sombrero de sol	som-brair-oh de sol
sunshade	el toldo	tol-doh
sunstroke	la insolación	een-so-la-**thyon**
suntan oil	el aceite para broncear	a-thay-te pa-ra bron-the-ar
supper	la cena	the-na
supplementary charge	el suplemento	soo-ple-men-toh
sure	seguro	se-goo-ro
surface mail	el correo ordinario	kor-ray-oh or-dee-na-ryo
surgery	la clínica	**klee**-nee-ka
suspender belt	el liguero	lee-gair-oh
sweater	el jersey	hair-say
sweet	dulce	dool-the
swell (to)	hinchar	een-char

swim (to)	nadar	na-dar
swimming pool	la piscina	pees-thee-na
switch *light*	la llave de la luz	llya-be de la looth
swollen	hinchado	een-cha-do

T

table	la mesa	me-sa
tablecloth	el mantel	man-tel
tablet	la pastilla	pas-tee-llya
tailor	el sastre	sas-tre
take (to)	tomar	toh-mar
talk (to)	hablar	ab-lar
tall	alto	al-toh
tap	el grifo	gree-fo
taste	el gusto	goos-toh
tax	el impuesto (de lujo)	eem-pwes-toh
taxi	el taxi	tak-see
taxi rank	la parada de taxis	pa-ra-da de tak-sees
tea	el té	te
teach (to)	enseñar	en-sen-yar
telegram	el telegrama	tele-grama
telephone (to)	telefonear	tele-fo-ne-ar
telephone	el teléfono	te-le-fo-no

telephone box	la cabina telefónica	ka-bee-na tele-**fo**-nee-ka
telephone call	la llamada telefónica	llya-ma-da tele-**fo**-nee-ka
telephone directory	la lista de teléfonos	lees-ta de te-**le**-fo-nos
telephone number	el número de teléfono	**noo**-mair-oh de te-**le**-fo-no
telephone operator	la telefonista	tele-fo-nee-sta
television	la televisión	tele-bee-**syon**
tell (to)	decir	de-theer
temperature	la temperatura	tem-pair-a-too-ra
tennis	el tenis	te-nees
tent	la tienda (de campaña)	tyen-da
tent peg	la estaquilla	es-ta-kee-llya
tent pole	el palo de la tienda	pa-lo de la tyen-da
terrace	la terraza	ter-ra-tha
than	que	ke
thank you	gracias	gra-thyas
that	ese	e-se
theatre	el teatro	te-a-tro
their	su	soo
then	entonces	en-ton-thes
there	allí	a-llyee

there is/are	hay	a-ee
thermometer	el termómetro	tair-**mo**-me-tro
these	estos	es-tos
they	ellos	ellyos
thick	grueso	grwe-so
thin	fino	fee-no
thing	la cosa	ko-sa
think (to)	pensar	pen-sar
thirsty (to be)	tener sed	te-nair se
this	este	es-te
those	aquellos	ake-llyos
thread	el hilo	ee-lo
throat	la garganta	gar-gan-ta
through	por	por
throw (to)	tirar	tee-rar
thumb	el pulgar	pool-gar
Thursday	jueves *m*	hwe-bes
ticket *train*	el billete	bee-llye-te
ticket *theatre*	la entrada	en-tra-da
tide	la marea	ma-re-a
tie	la corbata	kor-ba-ta
tight	ajustado	a-hoos-ta-doh
time	el tiempo, la hora	tyem-po, o-ra

timetable	el horario	orar-yo
tin	la lata	la-ta
tin opener	el abrelatas	abre-la-tas
tip	la propina	pro-pee-na
tip (to)	dar propina	dar pro-pee-na
tired (to be)	estar cansado	es-tar kan-sa-doh
tissues *paper*	los pañuelos de papel	pan-ywe-los de pa-pel
to	a	a
toast	la tostada	tos-ta-da
tobacco (brown, virginia)	el tabaco (negro, rubio)	ta-ba-ko (ne-gro, roo-byo)
tobacco pouch	la petaca	pe-ta-ka
tobacconist's	el estanco	es-tan-ko
today	hoy	oy
toe	el dedo del pie	de-doh del pee-ay
together	juntos	hoon-tos
toilet	los servicios	sair-bee-thyos
toilet paper	el papel higiénico	pa-pel ee-**hyen**-ee-ko
tomato	el tomate	to-ma-te
tomorrow	mañana	man-ya-na
tongue	la lengua	len-gwa
tonight	esta noche	es-ta no-che
too *also*	también	tam-**byen**

too, too much/many	demasiado	de-ma-sya-do
tooth	el diente	dyen-te
toothache	el dolor de muelas	do-lor de mwe-las
toothbrush	el cepillo de dientes	the-pee-llyo de dyen-tes
toothpaste	el dentífrico	den-tee-free-ko
toothpick	el palillo	pal-ee-llyo
top	la cima	thee-ma
torch	la linterna	leen-tair-na
torn	roto	ro-toh
touch (to)	tocar	toh-kar
tourist	el turista	too-rees-ta
towards	hacia	a-thya
towel	la toalla	toh-a-llya
tower	la torre	tor-re
town	la ciudad	thyoo-da
toy	el juguete	hoo-ge-te
traffic	el tráfico	**tra**-fee-ko
traffic jam	el taponamiento	ta-po-na-myen-toh
traffic lights	las luces de tráfico	loo-thes de **tra**-fee-ko
train	el tren	tren
translate (to)	traducir	tra-doo-theer
travel (to)	viajar	bya-har

travel agent	la agencia de viajes	ahen-thee-a de bya-hes
traveller	el viajero	bya-hair-oh
traveller's cheque	el cheque de viajero	che-ke de bya-hair-oh
treatment	el tratamiento	tra-ta-myen-toh
tree	el árbol	**ar**-bol
trip	el viaje	bya-he
trouble	la dificultad	dee-fee-kool-ta
trousers	los pantalones	pan-ta-lo-nes
true	verdad	bair-da
trunk *luggage*	el baúl	ba-**ool**
trunks *bathing*	el bañador	ban-ya-dor
try (to)	intentar	een-ten-tar
try on (to)	probarse	pro-bar-se
Tuesday	martes *m*	mar-tes
tunnel	el túnel	**too**-nel
turn (to)	dar la vuelta, volver	dar la bwel-ta, bol-bair
twisted	torcido	tor-thee-doh

U

ugly	feo	fe-oh
umbrella	el paraguas	pa-ra-gwas
(beach) umbrella	la sombrilla	som-bree-llya

uncle	el tío	**tee**-oh
uncomfortable	incómodo	een-**ko**-mo-doh
under	debajo (de)	de-ba-ho
underground	el metro	me-tro
understand	entender	en-ten-dair
underwater fishing	pesca submarina	pes-ka soob-mar-eena
underwear	la ropa interior	ro-pa een-ter-yor
university	la universidad	oo-nee-bair-see-da
until	hasta	as-ta
unusual	raro	ra-ro
up, upstairs	arriba	ar-ree-ba
urgent	urgente	oor-hen-te
use (to)	usar	oo-sar
usual	usual	oo-soo-al

V

vacant	libre	lee-bre
vaccination	la vacuna	ba-koo-na
valid	válido	**ba**-lee-doh
valley	el valle	ba-llye
valuable	valioso	bal-yo-so
value	el valor	ba-lor
vase	el florero	flo-rair-oh

veal	la ternera	tair-nair-a
vegetable	la legumbre	le-goom-bre
vegetarian	vegetariano	be-he-ta-rya-no
veil	el velo	be-lo
vein	la vena	be-na
ventilation	la ventilación	ben-tee-la-**thyon**
very	muy	mwee
very much	mucho	moo-cho
view	la vista	bees-ta
village	el pueblo	pwe-blo
vinegar	el vinagre	bee-na-gre
violin	el violín	byo-**leen**
visa	la visa	bee-sa
visit	la visita	bee-see-ta
visit (to)	visitar	bee-see-**tar**
voice	la voz	both
voltage	el voltaje	bol-ta-he
vomit (to)	devolver	de-bol-bair
voyage	el viaje	bya-he

W

wait (to)	esperar	es-pair-ar
waiter	el camarero	ka-ma-rair-oh

waiting room	la sala de espera	sa-la de es-pair-a
waitress	la camarera	ka-ma-rair-a
wake (to)	despertar	des-pair-tar
Wales	Gales *m*	ga-les
walk	el paseo	pa-se-oh
walk (to)	ir a pie, caminar	eer a pee-ay, ka-meen-ar
wallet	el billetero	bee-llye-tair-oh
want (to)	querer	ke-rair
wardrobe	el armario	ar-ma-ryo
warm *food, drink*	caliente	kal-yen-te
warm *weather*	cálido	**ka**-lee-doh
wash (to)	lavar	la-bar
washbasin	el lavabo	la-ba-boh
watch	el reloj	re-lo-h
water	el agua *f*	ag-wa
waterfall	la cascada	kas-ka-da
water melon	la sandía	san-**dee**-a
water ski-ing	el esquí acuático	es-kee a-**kwa**-tee-ko
wave	la ola	o-la
way	el camino	ka-mee-no
we	nosotros	no-so-tros

wear (to)	llevar	llye-bar
weather	el tiempo	tyem-po
Wednesday	miércoles *m*	**myair**-ko-les
week	la semana	se-ma-na
weigh (to)	pesar	pe-sar
well	bien	byen
Welsh	galés	ga-**les**
west	el oeste	wes-te
wet	húmedo	**oo**-me-doh
what ?	¿qué ?	ke
wheel	la rueda	rwe-da
when ?	¿cuándo ?	kwan-doh
where ?	¿dónde ?	don-de
which ?	¿cuál ?	kwal
while	mientras	myen-tras
white	blanco	blan-ko
who ?	¿quién ?	kyen
whole	todo	toh-doh
whose ?	¿de quién ?	de kyen
why ?	¿por qué ?	por ke
wide	ancho	an-cho
widow	la viuda	byoo-da
widower	el viudo	byoo-doh

wife	la mujer	moo-hair
win (to)	ganar	ga-nar
wind	el viento	byen-toh
window	la ventana	ben-ta-na
wine	el vino	bee-noh
wine list	la lista de vinos	lees-ta de bee-nos
winter	invierno	een-byair-noh
wish (to)	desear	de-se-ar
with	con	kon
without	sin	seen
woman	la mujer	moo-hair
wool	la lana	la-na
word	la palabra	pa-la-bra
worse	peor	pe-or
worth (to be)	valer	ba-lair
wound	la herida	eree-da
wrap	envolver	en-bol-bair
wrist	la muñeca	moon-ye-ka
write (to)	escribir	es-kree-beer
writing paper	el papel de escribir	pa-pel de es-kree-beer
wrong	equivocado	ekee-bo-ka-doh

X

X ray	la radiografía	ra-dyo-gra-**fee**-a

Y

yacht	el yate	ya-te
year	el año	an-yo
yellow	amarillo	ama-ree-llyo
yes	sí	see
yesterday	ayer	a-yair
you	usted	oos-te
young	joven	ho-ben
your	su	soo
youth hostel	el albergue juvenil	al-bair-ge hoo-be-neel

Z

zip	la cremallera	kre-ma-llye-ra
zoo	el (parque) zoológico	par-ke thoo-o-**lo**-hee-ko

Notes

Notes

Notes

Notes